Come *on* Home

✣ ✣

❖

HEALING THE
HOMESICKNESS *of the* SOUL

Come *on* Home

JAMES W. MOORE

Abingdon Press / *Nashville*

COME *on* HOME

HEALING THE HOMESICKNESS OF THE SOUL

This book is printed on acid-free paper.

Library of Congress Cataloging-in-Publication Data

Moore, James W. (James Wendell), 1938-
    Come on home : healing the homesickness of the soul / James W. Moore.
        p. cm.
    Includes bibliographical references and index.
    ISBN 978-1-4267-5329-9 (book - pbk. / trade pbk. : alk. paper) 1. Spirituality. I. Title.
    BV4501.3.M656   2012
    248.4—dc23

                                                                                          2012027600

12 13 14 15 16 17 18 19 20 21—10 9 8 7 6 5 4 3 2 1

MANUFACTURED IN THE UNITED STATES OF AMERICA

In memory of my former pastors and teachers, to whom I owe so much, who each in his or her own unique way inspired me greatly, taught me dramatically, and encouraged me faithfully to come home to God

✤ ✤ ✤ ✤ ✤ ✤ ✤ ✤ ✤ ✤ ✤ ✤ ✤ ✤ ✤ ✤ ✤ ✤ ✤ ✤

Contents

❧ ❧

Come on Home
(The Homing Instinct)

I am so impressed with the miraculous technology of our time. I am even more in awe of a phenomenon that happens year after year on March 19. Do you have any idea what I'm talking about? For more than two hundred years, on March 19, the swallows have faithfully returned to the southern California city of San Juan Capistrano on exactly that day! They will do it again next year. March 19 is officially the last day of winter. Spring begins each year on March 20, whether there is snow on the ground and the temperatures are below freezing, or whether the skies are balmy and temperatures are in the high 80s. March 19 marks the end of winter, and March 20 begins the spring season. And somehow, miraculously, these little birds "know" that March 19 is the day for them to return to Capistrano. How do they know this? I mean, every four years there is a leap year, when instead of there being twenty-eight days in February, there are twenty-nine, but apparently this doesn't faze those little swallows at all. They somehow know how to compute that subtle difference and to show up again on exactly March 19. It's phenomenal, really—one of the great mysteries and marvels of God's creation that no one understands. They just come home!

Recently, as I was thinking of this, I realized that deep down inside of us there is a "homing instinct." There is something deep down inside of us that just hungers and thirsts for home. Whether we realize it or not, we all yearn to come home to God. That is precisely what Psalm 42 is all about, and this is what Saint Augustine was talking about when he wrote what has become his most famous quotation: "My soul is restless, O God, till it finds its rest in Thee."

The hymn writers of our faith realize this truth, and often they write of "coming home" to be with God. Remember the words from the famous gospel hymn: "Softly and tenderly, Jesus is calling, calling for you and for me. . . . Come home, come home; you who are weary come home."

As a minister, I spend a lot of time in cemeteries, and over the years I have noticed something that is fascinating and revealing. The inscriptions on gravestone markers have a great deal to teach us. As you look at these gravestones, you notice how many say things like:

"Beloved Wife and Mother"
"Devoted Dad"
"Husband and Father"
"Parents of Scott, Debra, & Mary Ann"
"Our Darling Daughter"
"Faithful Friend"
"The Best Mother of All"
"God's Servant"

Interestingly, nowhere on any grave marker have I ever read "Popular Writer" or "Successful Banker" or "Rich and Famous."

And the point is clear and crucial. When the end came and these people's lives were reduced to a few words on a piece of granite, those words almost invariably referred to relationships they had built and the love they had left behind. And the lesson for us is obvious. We can make a lot of money, develop clout, hold offices, wield influence, sit in high places—and still be perfectly miserable if our relationships are not right. I am more convinced now than ever that happiness, fulfillment, meaning, purpose, and peace of mind come not from material things or accomplishments, but from right relationships, from being "at home" in our relationships. If our relationships are out of whack, everything in our life is out of whack—distorted, strained, smudged, stressed, unhappy, unfulfilled, and empty.

The New Testament (and uniquely the Sermon on the Mount) makes it dramatically clear: happiness is the by-product of being in right relationship with God and with other people, of being "at home" with God and with others. On more than one occasion, Jesus reminded us that the Great Commandment is to love God and to love other people. And that is what Matthew 6:33 is all about: "Seek first [God's] kingdom and his righteousness, and all these things will be given to you as well" (NIV). Notice the word "righteousness" here. In the theology of the New Testament, the word "righteousness" doesn't just mean doing the right thing; it also means being in right relationship with God and our neighbors. It means being right-wised or set right with God and with other people. This is a crucial concept all through the New Testament. We see it strongly repeated in the teachings of Jesus and underscored over and over in the letters of the apostle Paul: the importance of relationships, the significance of being at peace and "at home" with God and with our neighbors.

Recently, on a lengthy airplane trip, I was reading a newspaper when, inadvertently, I noticed those personal ads in the back of the classified section. A lot of people with initials are telling unnamed persons that they are forgiven: "You are forgiven and you can come home," they say. Evidently, they know who they are. "You can come home now. Please come home now. You are forgiven." As I read these poignant messages, it occurred to me that that's what the cross means—and it reminded me of that story about the policeman who one day found a little boy sitting on the curb in the downtown section of a big city. The little boy was crying because he was lost. The policeman said: "Don't you worry. I'll help you find your way home. Glance around and see if you can see anything that looks familiar to you." The little boy looked around for a few moments, and then suddenly his face brightened because off in the distance he could see a church. It had a tall steeple with a cross on top of it, and it was familiar to him. Then the little boy said: "There! Look! If you can get me to the cross, we can find the way home from there!"

That is what the cross does for us. It brings us home to God. There is an empty spot in our hearts and lives that only God can fill. God was in Christ reconciling the world to himself. God was on the cross reconciling the world to himself. God was on the cross bringing us home—and that is precisely where we are all meant to be: at home with God and at home with our neighbors!

✤ ✤

CHAPTER 1

Come on Home to Faith

Scripture: Romans 12:1-13

Just last week, I saw a bumper sticker that fascinated me. It read like this: "What do you mean we don't communicate anymore? Just yesterday I faxed you a reply to the recorded message you left on my telephone answering machine!"

Communication is so important. The way we communicate can bring joy or sorrow, encouragement or discouragement, hate or love, peace or war, healing or sickness, harmony or discord.

The power and significance of communication is seen dramatically in the Helen Keller story. In the spring of 1887, seven-year-old Helen Keller was a deaf, blind, and frightening creature who terrified the life out of almost everyone who came near her. She was like an angry, violent animal—out of control. She would utter unintelligible, scary, guttural sounds. In a rage, she would smash dishes against the wall. She would turn chairs over, throw food, and knock things off the dinner table. She would pitch fits, flinging herself on the floor, kicking and screaming and slapping at anyone who came close.

The conclusion of many people was that seven-year-old Helen Keller was an idiot. And by the way she was acting, there wasn't much reason, back in those days, to doubt that conclusion. Then along came a twenty-year-old teacher named Anne Sullivan. Anne Sullivan arrived at the Keller home in Tuscumbia, Alabama, and immediately began to try to communicate with little Helen Keller. Anne believed she could break through to Helen by spelling words in her hands. The key was to help Helen understand that things have names!

For weeks and weeks she tried, but to no avail. Helen couldn't understand, she couldn't comprehend what Anne was trying to communicate. Finally, on April 5, the big breakthrough occurred. They were at the wellhouse. Helen was holding a coffee mug under a water spout. Anne Sullivan pumped water into the mug—and when the water spilled over onto Helen's hand, Anne continued to spell "w-a-t-e-r" into Helen's other hand. "Feel that? It has a name. Water is its name. W-a-t-e-r. That is water!"

Suddenly, the lightbulb turned on for Helen Keller. She understood! She grabbed Anne Sullivan's ever-ready hand and begged for more words. A whole new exciting world had opened for Helen. She became a new and beautiful person. Anne spent most of her life with Helen Keller. She went to college with Helen, sitting by her through every class at Radcliffe.

Helen went on to become the friend of kings and princes and presidents and an inspiration to the whole world. All because a young teacher cared for this little, scared, difficult, frustrated child. All because Anne Sullivan helped Helen Keller understand that things have names—and when you understand the names, a whole new world opens up to you. When you understand the names, you can communicate.

This is true in every dimension of life, but it is especially true spiritually. In the world of faith it helps so much to know the words of faith; it helps to know the names. Let me show you what I mean by sharing with you three true stories.

❧ ❧ ❧ ❧ ❧

THE FIRST STORY

The first story is about a minister who went some years ago to be the pastor in a church in a little village in East Tennessee called Watts Bar Dam. It was the custom of that little church to have a baptismal service each year at Easter. Those who wanted to be baptized were immersed in Watts Bar Lake on Easter evening at sundown.

The minister would lead the candidates for baptism out on a sandbar first and then into the water. After they were baptized, they would come together back to the shore, where the little congregation of folk who had been watching were now singing hymns and cooking supper. They would have constructed little booths, made with ropes and posts and hanging blankets, where the newly baptized could change into dry clothes. And after they moved out of the water and changed clothes, they would go warm themselves by the fire in the center of the gathering.

Once the people were all gathered by the fire, this was the ritual of that tradition: one of the leading laymen would introduce the new members. He would give their names, tell where they lived, and describe their work.

Then, the rest of the small congregation would form a tight circle around the newly baptized folk, while they stayed warm by the fire. The tradition was that all the church members in the circle would then introduce themselves to the new members. Going round the circle, each would speak in turn like this:

"My name is Tom. If you ever need anyone to chop wood for you, call on me."

"My name is Thelma. If you ever need anyone to do washing and ironing, I'm pretty good at it."

"My name is Andy. If you ever need anyone to repair your house, I'm available and I can fix most anything."

"My name is Sheila. If you ever need anyone to babysit, give me a ring. I love children."

"My name is Mary. If you ever need anyone to sit with the sick, call me. I'm not a registered nurse, but I've had a lot of experience in the sick-room and I know how to handle most any situation."

"My name is Willard. If you ever need a ride to town, just give a holler and I'll come pick you up."

And so on around the circle it went until every member of the church had spoken a welcome to the new members and offered them their friendship and help.

Then the people ate and played folk games and sang songs and visited and made the new members feel wanted and included. Finally, at a certain time only they knew, another leading layman would stand up and, with thumbs at the top of his bibbed overalls, say: "It's time to go."

And everybody would go to their cars and pickup trucks and head for home. The minister would linger behind with one of the laymen. With his big farm shoe, the layman would kick sand over the dying fire and then, turning to the pastor, would say the same thing every year: "Reverend, folks don't ever get any closer than this."

Now, there's a name for that: It's called *church*. (Story adapted from *Craddock Stories* by Fred B. Craddock, Mike Graves, and Richard F. Ward, eds. [St. Louis: Chalice Press, 2001], 151–52.)

❦ ❦ ❦ ❦ ❦

THE SECOND STORY

This story happened more recently. Another minister friend of mine tells about being visited one day by some of his top church leaders. "It's

Mrs. Barnett," they told him. "She's getting up in years now and she loves our church. She's living all alone in that big, beautiful house on the west side of town. She has no relatives. So we want you as our minister to go to her and ask her to give her house to the church."

My minister friend gulped! He had never done anything like that before. How do you ask someone to give you their house? He was scared to death. He was embarrassed. He didn't want to do that. But the church officials persisted. "You've got to do it. No one else can. You're the pastor. It would be such a wonderful thing for our church if Mrs. Barnett would leave us her house. Now, you go ask her!"

The minister dreaded the thought of that. He felt so inadequate and afraid. He took his wife along for support. Mrs. Barnett was most gracious and welcomed them warmly. She took them into the living room and served them tea and cookies. The minister was so nervous that he did everything wrong. He accidentally kicked the coffee table, he spilled his tea just a little bit, and he dropped cookie crumbs on the elegant carpet. He was so discombobulated.

Finally, the minister got up his courage. He took a deep breath, cleared his throat, and just blurted it out: "Some of us at the church were wondering if you would consider giving your house to the church." There was absolute silence. No response. Nothing is more silent than that. You ask somebody to give you their house, and they don't respond. Now, that is silence.

By now, the minister was so flustered that he tried to say a prayer. He, his wife, and Mrs. Barnett held hands in a circle and the minister prayed. As he prayed, he noticed that over and over his wife kept squeezing his hand. There was urgency in that squeeze. The minister knew he was doing something wrong and his wife was trying to signal him; but, for the life of him, he couldn't figure out what it was.

Just as he finished his prayer, it hit him. All the way through the prayer he had been calling Mrs. Barnett by the wrong name! Several different times in his prayer, he had called her Mrs. Bennett. As soon as he said the "Amen" of his prayer, Mrs. Barnett said: "Now, I would like to pray"; and with a little smile she bowed her head and said, "Dear Lord, my name is Barnett not Bennett, but of course, O Lord, you know that even if my minister doesn't. Amen."

The minister was so embarrassed. He apologized and apologized profusely, but the damage had been done. He and his wife drove home in silence. Finally he said, "That was absolutely awful! How could I do that? I know her name like I know my own, but I was so rattled I blew it. She's probably going to leave the church, and who would blame her? I ought to quit the ministry, I ought to just give it up. I failed so miserably—I failed the church and I failed her. How could God ever forgive me? I'm so ashamed and so embarrassed."

Three days later, Mrs. Barnett called, and she said: "Well, Reverend, I decided you're right. I've been thinking about it and you're right. I have no living relatives and leaving my house to the church would be a beautiful thing to do. It would help the church so much, and I would feel so good about that. My lawyer is on the way over now to draw up the papers."

"But I don't understand," said the minister. "I did everything wrong!"

"That's just it," said Mrs. Barnett. "I felt so sorry for you. I think you need all the help you can get."

Now, there's a name for that: it's called *grace*. Grace—it's the break that comes our way when we have done absolutely nothing to deserve it. That's the simple explanation, but the truth is we don't really understand grace till we experience it like that, firsthand.

❧ ❧ ❧ ❧ ❧

THE THIRD STORY

This next story is about a pastor who performed a marriage ceremony for a fine young couple. They were so much in love and had a bright future ahead of them. The groom was a farmer, and a very good one at that.

Shortly after the birth of their third child, however, his wife developed what turned out to be an incurable disease. After an incredible number of examinations, which pretty well depleted their financial resources, she was diagnosed as having terminal cancer. She was told that it was a slow-growing malignancy and therefore she would have some quality of life, but it would be limited.

On their tenth wedding anniversary, the couple invited their pastor and his wife over to have dinner with them to celebrate the occasion (probably their last one). The minister noticed that the farm wasn't anything like it used to be. Much of the equipment had been sold. When they sat down to dinner, it was obvious that there was very little food to be shared, but there was plenty of love around the table. The husband took care of his wife and three children with such great tenderness.

After a while, the minister and his wife stood to leave. However, the farmer asked them if they would wait just a moment because he wanted them to see the anniversary present he had for his wife. He told his wife to close her eyes. He went into the bedroom and came back with a thin, flat package. It turned out to be a gorgeous string of pearls—and they were the real McCoy.

With her eyes still closed, the wife felt her husband fasten the pearls around her neck. She knew immediately what they were and reached up and touched them gently without opening her eyes. Then she burst into tears, saying that she knew they could not possibly be for her. The farmer then told this incredible story:

"You know, honey, before we were married you said you thought pearls were the prettiest jewelry in the entire world. You thought they were prettier than any other jewelry except your wedding band. Well, a long time before we were married, I asked the Lord to help me put this string of pearls around your neck. I started dropping nickels and dimes into a secret place. I gave up tobacco and sodas, and for thirteen years (the three before we married and the ten years we've been married) I've been saving nickels and dimes and quarters in that old shoebox, just waiting for this moment. And now I have been able to buy these pearls for you, and I can tell you that they are real and they're completely paid for!"

Overcome by this, she asked, "Joe, what made you do it? What on earth made you do it?" He knelt down beside her and began to weep. The pastor and his wife quietly slipped out of the room, but as they left they could hear the husband say to her, "I did it because I'm crazy about you! I've been crazy about you since the first moment I saw you."

Now, there's a name for that: it's called *love*.

You may be thinking, *When in the world are we going to get to the Scripture lesson? When are we going to get to Romans 12?* Well, the truth is that Romans 12 has been with us all along. We've been thinking together about church and grace and love, which is precisely what Romans 12 is all about. Here Paul is giving the people of Rome his personal statement of faith. Look again at his powerful words.

First, he says: "I appeal to you therefore, brothers and sisters, by the mercies of God, to present your bodies as a living sacrifice, holy and acceptable to God, which is your spiritual worship. . . . So we, who are many, are one body in Christ. . . . We have gifts that differ according to the grace given to us: prophecy . . . ministry . . . teaching . . . exhortation . . . generosity . . . diligence . . . cheerfulness" (vv. 1, 5-8). Listen! There's a name for that: It's called *church*.

Next, Paul says: "For by the grace given to me I say to everyone among you not to think of yourself more highly than you ought to think, but to think with sober judgment, each according to the measure of faith that God has assigned" (v. 3). Listen! There's a name for that: it's called *grace*!

Finally, Paul says, "Let love be genuine . . . love one another with mutual affection; outdo one another in showing honor. Do not lag in zeal, be ardent in spirit, serve the Lord. Rejoice in hope, be patient in suffering, persevere in prayer. Contribute to the needs of [others]; extend hospitality to strangers" (vv. 9-13). Listen! There's a name for that: it's called *love*!

Powerful words for those early Christians—and for us today. Do you know what Paul is talking about here in Romans 12? He is talking about continuing Christ's ministry in this world. He is talking about being God's people, God's servants, God's instruments. He's talking about church and grace and love. He is talking about coming home to God.

❧ ❧

CHAPTER 2

Come on Home to God's Greatest Promise

Scripture: Psalm 139:7-12

Just last week, a good friend put a cartoon on my desk that impressed me. It shows a little girl named Mikki walking down the sidewalk with her mother. They are holding hands. As they walk along, little Mikki asks: "Mommy, what is God?" The mother answers: "Well, Mikki, God is the Creative Force, the First Cause, the Unmoved Mover, the Unseen

Primal Cause of Existence, the Binding, Sentient Energy that underpins physical manifestations, the . . ." At that point, the little girl interrupts, "Mommy, Mommy, Wait! Use words that are my size. Tell me, Mommy, what is God?"

Mom takes a deep breath and tries again. "Really, Mikki, it's hard to explain. God's like all the good stuff, the essence of all the beauty around us. God is—well—God is . . ." Mikki realizes that her mom is struggling. She helps out by saying, "Mommy, I think God is love!" Her mom smiles, hugs her, and says, "That just proves one thing, Mikki. You are smarter than most of the adults I know." Mikki, in her childlike way, had put her finger on the good news of our faith. God is love; God is our friend; God cares about us; God is on our side; and God will never desert us.

A noted journalist told about a time some years ago when he was at the breaking point. He was physically exhausted, emotionally drained, under severe nervous strain, confused, perplexed, stressed out, not knowing which way to turn concerning some highly important decisions he had to make. He was staying at a friend's house prior to speaking at a big meeting. His friend said to him, "You look tired; would you like to escape all this chatter, and rest in a room upstairs?" The journalist said that he would like that very much. To his delight, he was led to a beautiful, peaceful room, a bright fire was burning, an easy chair was drawn up near the hearth, and at his elbow there was a little table with a Bible on it.

The Bible was open at Psalm 59, and in the margin opposite verse 10 someone had written in pencil a fascinating interpretation that kindled his mind and warmed his heart (as it does my own). In the King James

Version, Psalm 59:10 reads like this: "The God of my mercy shall prevent me." Let me hurry to say that in Old English the word *prevent* means "go before." But the penciled interpretation in the margin read like this: "My God in his lovingkindness shall meet me at every corner."

The journalist said that when he read those words the message came to him as light in a dark place, light from the very heart of God. It lifted him, consoled him, encouraged him, revitalized him—and gave him the strength and courage to make his decisions and do what had to be done. "My God in his lovingkindness shall meet me at every corner." That is our faith, our hope, our confidence. That is the overriding theme of the Bible. And that is what our Scripture lesson for this chapter is all about: "God in his lovingkindness meeting us at every corner." Look again at these magnificent words in Psalm 139:

> Whither shall I go from thy spirit?
>> or whither shall I flee from thy presence?
> If I ascend up into heaven, thou art there;
>> if I make my bed in hell, behold, thou art there.
> If I take the wings of the morning,
>> and dwell in the uttermost parts of the sea;
> Even there shall thy hand lead me,
>> and thy right hand shall hold me.
> If I say, Surely the darkness shall cover me;
>> even the night shall be light about me.
> Yea, the darkness hideth not from thee;
>> but the night shineth as the day:
> the darkness and the light are both alike to thee." (139:7-12 KJV)

Powerful words, incredible words that represent one of the highest peaks in all of the Bible.

Recently, I received a letter from one of our church members. In it, she had a line that sums this all up. She wrote: "There is no spot where God is not." This is indeed what the psalmist is saying, isn't it? No matter what kind of trouble or heartache or darkness we have to pass through—God is there. There is no spot where God is not; God meets us at every corner with lovingkindness. Now, let's bring this closer to home and be more specific.

❦ ❦ ❦ ❦ ❦

FIRST, AT THE PLACE OF REJECTION, GOD IS THERE FOR US

Let me ask you something. Have you ever felt rejected, shunned, pushed aside, abused, not accepted, deserted? All of us at one time or another have felt the awful pain of rejection. It is without question one of the most hurtful, agonizing, devastating experiences in life. That phrase in Psalm 139, "the uttermost parts of the sea," means "the dropping-off place." (Remember, back then they thought the world was flat, and if you got to that totally remote place in the sea, you would drop off the face of the earth.) And when we feel rejected or deserted—that's about as harsh a dropping-off place as there is.

Some years ago, a priest was kidnapped and spent many long, horrible months as a prisoner of Lebanese terrorists. Since his release, he has often told of the awful abuse and the inhumane treatment that he and others endured. He tells of how one day he was bound and trussed like a turkey and shoved onto a rack beneath a flatbed truck where the spare tire is usually stored. Apparently his captors were taking him to a new hideout. The priest felt certain that they were taking him out to kill him.

As he took that awful ride, he remembers what gave him the courage to face that moment. He kept saying these words to himself, "I am a human being of worth and dignity. I belong to God. I am redeemed. I am a child of God. He cares for me and nothing can separate me from him and his love." He prayed over and over these familiar words: "Yea, though I walk through the valley of the shadow of death, I will fear no evil; for thou art with me" (Psalm 23:4 KJV). Again and again, he spoke aloud the strong words of Jesus: "Lo, I am with you alway" (Matthew 28:20 KJV). Later, he said, those promises of God "to be with us in every circumstance" kept him alive and sane and hopeful.

It is very unlikely that any of us will ever have to go through that kind of traumatic experience, that kind of blatant abuse; but we all know what rejection feels like—and how painful it is. When it comes, when it happens, when we feel cast out to the uttermost parts of the sea, to the dropping-off place, the good news is that God will be there for us, even there with God's special brand of love, grace, encouragement, and acceptance. When you feel rejected, remember that you are God's child, you are a person of integrity and worth. God loves you, claims you, accepts you, and if somebody else doesn't, that's their problem; they are the ones with the problem. The rejecters are the ones with the problem, because you cannot reject people and live in the spirit of God. You cannot abuse people and live in the spirit of God. The spirit of God is grace and love and acceptance.

❧ ❧ ❧ ❧ ❧

SECOND, AT THE PLACE OF TROUBLE, THE PLACE OF DARKNESS, GOD IS THERE FOR US

One of the most effective and colorful Congressmen to ever go to Washington was a crusty old gentleman from Texas. His name was Sam Rayburn. He served in Congress for more than fifty years, the last ten or more as Speaker of the House. But the real greatness of Sam Rayburn was not in the public positions he held. It was in his common touch.

One day he heard that the teenage daughter of a Washington reporter had died. Early the next morning he went over to that reporter's house and knocked on the door. "I just came by to see what I could do to help," he said. The reporter, obviously touched, said, "Well, thank you, Mr. Speaker, but I don't think there's anything you can do. We're handling all the arrangements." "Let me ask you something," said Sam Rayburn. "Have you had your coffee yet this morning?" When the reporter said that he had not, Mr. Sam said, "Well, I'll make it for you." And into the house he went. As Mr. Sam was fixing the coffee in the kitchen, the reporter said, "Mr. Speaker, I thought you were having breakfast this morning at the White House with the president." Mr. Rayburn said, "Well, I was. But I called the president and told him that I had a friend who was having some trouble and that I wouldn't be in today."

Now, that incident—that act of kindness, that spirit—must have made God smile because that is so akin to the nature of God. God is with us always, but somehow God comes even closer to us when we are in trouble. The 139th Psalm tells how God brings light to our darkness. Interestingly, when the psalmist wrote these words, many of the peoples of that day believed their gods were powerless at night. But our God (said the psalmist) overwhelms the darkness with the light of God's love. Even in the darkness—indeed, especially in the darkness—God is there for us.

"Footprints in the Sand," a poem by Mary Stevenson that is becoming a classic, underscores this.

The poem tells the story of a man who one night had a dream. He dreamed he was walking along the beach with the Lord. Across the sky flashed scenes from his life; for each scene he noticed two sets of footprints in the sand—one belonging to him, the other to the Lord. When the last scene of his life flashed before him, he looked back at the footprints in the sand. Then he noticed that many times along the path of his life there was only one set of footprints. He also noticed that it happened at the very lowest and saddest times of his life.

That really bothered the man, and he questioned the Lord about it. "Lord, you said that once I decided to follow you, you'd walk with me all the way. But I have noticed that during the most troublesome times in my life there is only one set of footprints. I don't understand why in times when I needed you most you would leave me." The Lord replied, "Oh, my precious, precious child, I love you and would never leave you; during your times of trials and suffering, when you see only one set of footprints, it was then that I carried you."

We can count on it. The Bible makes it clear—God will always be there for us, at the uttermost parts of the sea, the dropping-off place, the place of rejection, and the places of darkness—the valleys, the shadows, the trouble spots.

🌱 🌱 🌱 🌱 🌱

THIRD, AND FINALLY, EVEN AT THE PLACE OF DEATH, GOD IS THERE

The word *Sheol* is a difficult one to translate. It means the pit or the place of death. Each year on Memorial Day weekend, we remember with love those who have given their lives for our country and our freedom; indeed, we remember all our loved ones who have died.

At many churches and cemeteries (especially out in the country) people will be celebrating Decoration Day (the original name for Memorial Day). Folk will come from far and near to decorate the graves of their loved ones with flowers. The flowers are symbols of new life and resurrection and the good news of our faith, that nothing (not even death) can separate us from God and God's love. That's what the psalmist is talking about here. If I make my bed in Sheol, if I just fall down and die, God will even be there for me, at the place of death.

Some years ago, a young minister was devastated by the sudden death of his seven-year-old son. The staggering blow left him in the depths of despair. One day while out for a walk, he came to a beautiful estate. He saw a little girl (about five or six years old) come running out through an iron gate. She closed the gate behind her. Suddenly she realized that she had locked herself out. She began to cry and beat on the gate hysterically. Quickly, her mother came running to the little girl. She opened the gate, took the little girl in her arms, carried her back inside, and comforted her, saying, "Everything is all right, honey. You know I wouldn't leave you out here all alone. You know how much I love you. You knew I would come, didn't you?"

As the minister saw that young mother coming to rescue her daughter, he remembered that God is like that. No matter what the situation is, even at the place of death, "God is there for us." And the minister said, "In that moment, I saw with my spirit that there was love behind my shut gate also."

This is the hope, the confidence, the blessed assurance the psalmist is underscoring for us—that at the dropping-off place, at the place of darkness, and even at the place of death, God is there for us, meeting us with loving-kindness at every corner because there is no spot where God is not! The point is clear: wherever you find yourself, you can know with strong confidence that God is there with you—even in the deepest, darkest valleys of life. So come on home to God. Recognize God's presence, accept God's love, and feel God's grace.

❧ ❧

CHAPTER 3

Come on Home to Commitment

Scripture: Romans 12:1-2

On a recent trip to a shopping mall here in Texas, I saw an impressive demonstration of "Teflon Cookware." The salesman was quite a showman as he dramatically portrayed how effectively and easily you can cook an omelet in a Teflon skillet. He would drop the ingredients for the omelet into the Teflon skillet, swirl the mixture about quickly, cook it just a bit, then tilt the skillet. And very smoothly, the finished omelet would slide out the other side onto a platter. The key point in his sales pitch, which he repeated over and over, was this: "Nothing Will Stick to Teflon!"

As I watched his presentation, three thoughts came into my mind.

❧ ❧ ❧ ❧ ❧

FIRST, I THOUGHT OF THE DANGER
OF THE TEFLON MIND

As I watched the salesman's fascinating demonstration, which he performed with great fanfare, I found myself wondering if some of us have "Teflon minds," that is, minds to which nothing really sticks. We hear great truths, we are exposed to important lessons for living, we are taught significant life principles; but do they stick? do they take root? do they really become deeply ingrained within? do they become part of us? Or do we just swirl them about, cook them a little, then tilt the mind and let them slide off the other side? How is it with you? Do you have a "Teflon mind"?

Let me give you a dramatic illustration of what I'm talking about. Not long ago I ran across the story of a teenage girl named Martha who has been touring the country warning other teenagers about the dangers of hitchhiking. Martha looks like a normal, vivacious teenager, except that she has a heavy brace on her leg, causing her to walk with a pronounced limp, and her right arm is paralyzed, hanging dead weight to her side. Martha did not always have these physical handi-caps, but she is dealing with them quite well now. Indeed, she feels lucky to be alive.

One spring, after a spat with her parents, Martha ran away from home. Although she had been taught all her life about the dangers of hitchhik-ing, she ignored that advice, went to the highway, and hitched a ride. Subsequently she was kidnapped, robbed, beaten, and left for dead on the side of the highway. She survived the attack, but for the rest of her life she will have a paralyzed arm and a bad leg.

Now, she is going around the country telling her graphic story and then saying to other teenagers: "Don't hitchhike! It's dangerous! Look what happened to me. I'm lucky to be alive." She concludes her remarks by saying, "I had been warned all my life, people had told me hitchhiking was dangerous, but I didn't listen. It went in one ear and out the other."

Do you see what Martha is saying? She is saying, in effect, that she had a Teflon mind. She had heard about the dangers, but that lesson had not sunk in. It just slid off the other side—slid off, like an omelet sliding out of a Teflon skillet.

The terrible thing that happened to Martha is a gruesome reminder of the dangers of the Teflon mind. When nothing sticks in our minds to give us guidance and direction, then we are at the mercy of the latest propaganda, gossip, hysteria, fad, or personal whim. When we jump on bandwagons without regard for principles or run from fad to fad without regard for the purposes of God; when we are disloyal in our personal relationships or close our minds to the teachings of the church; when we say "Lord, Lord," but do not do the will of our Father in heaven—then (no question about it) we have a Teflon mind, and that is dangerous and destructive.

❧ ❧ ❧ ❧ ❧

SECOND, I THOUGHT OF THE POWER OF COMMITMENT

Our Scripture lesson for this chapter is the opposite of the Teflon mind. This passage, Romans 12:1-2, is one of the mountain peaks of the New Testament. When I was a young Christian, it was one of the first passages I was asked to memorize: "I appeal to you therefore . . . by the mercies of God, to present your bodies as a living sacrifice, holy and acceptable to God, which is your spiritual worship. Do not be conformed to this world, but be transformed by the renewing of your minds, so that you may discern what is the will of God—what is good and acceptable and perfect."

In other words, don't have a wishy-washy Teflon mind to which nothing sticks; rather, commit your life (all that you are and all that you have) to God and God's truth! The J. B. Phillips's translation of the New Testament says it like this: "Give [God] your bodies, as a living sacrifice, consecrated to him. . . . Don't let the world around you squeeze you into its own mould, but let God re-mould your minds from within, so that you may prove in practice that the plan of God for you is good" (12:1-2 Phillips).

Each year in the fall we celebrate All Saints Day, the Sunday traditionally set aside by the church to remember with love and gratitude the lives of our members who have died since this time last year. As we stand in silent tribute in the service and hear those names read aloud, I am always moved and touched again just remembering those special people. So many of them so beautifully exemplified our text, Romans 12:1-2. They gave themselves to God as living sacrifices totally consecrated to God.

Some on that list were great leaders; others were great followers. Some were high profile; others were quiet supporters. Some on that list started our church right; others kept it going. Some sat always near the front; others sat always near the back. Some were charter members, others had joined only recently. Some on the list were with us for a long time, influencing us in special ways over many years; others died too quickly, too tragically, and we weren't ready to give them up. Some died peacefully in their sleep; others died courageously, inspiring us with their faith, hope, strength, and serenity. But they all died as they lived—consecrated to God.

❧ ❧ ❧ ❧ ❧

THIRD, I THOUGHT OF THE BEST TRIBUTE WE CAN PAY JESUS CHRIST

Some years ago, Red Auerbach was the coach of the Boston Celtics basketball team. One day at practice, the players got a bit sloppy and careless. They were passing the ball behind their backs and doing fancy spin passes—and kept missing or dropping the passes. Four straight times down the floor, someone muffed a pass. Coach Auerbach blew his whistle and called the players over to him and asked for the ball. He then threw the ball to his center, Bill Russell, and Russell caught it. Then Coach Auerbach said: "You see that! A good pass is one that's caught." No matter how great a pass you throw, if no one catches it, it's not worth anything. No matter how great a lesson you teach or sermon you preach, if no one catches it, it's not worth anything.

If your pass only falls on Teflon minds, we are in big trouble. The real Christians are those who caught the pass. They caught it. It stuck. It took. They did their part. And now they pass the ball to us. We need to catch the pass. Listen! The best tribute we can pay Jesus Christ our Lord, the best tribute we can pay these saints who went before us, is to take up the torch of what they believed in and stood for and hold it high and carry it forward.

Recently as I thought of some of the Christians who have inspired and influenced me the most, I found myself thinking of three special qualities that they exemplified. We dare not have Teflon minds or Teflon hands, with regard to these qualities. We need to catch the pass. Now, here they are—three Christian qualities that need to stick and take root in our lives—the spirit of love, generosity, and commitment. To live sacrificially for God is to live in the spirit of love, generosity, and commitment.

Recently, I went on a speaking engagement at one of the best churches in America, a church that has a great Sunday school program and that has had a long series of truly outstanding preachers. While I was there, a woman asked if she might visit with me. In our conversation she immediately began to spew out ugly, harsh criticisms of everything and everybody. Her words were heavily coated with hostility and venom. She was so hateful toward her family and her church. I asked, "How long have you been a member of this church?" She answered: "Forty-two years, and I never miss. I'm here every Sunday for Sunday school and church."

I thought to myself: *Lady, haven't you been listening? All of these great preachers, all of those outstanding Sunday school teachers, all of the sermons and lessons and messages about love, grace, and kindness. Evidently they didn't take; they didn't stick. How can you go to a great church like that for forty-two years and miss the point? How could you participate in a great church like that for forty-two years and still be so hateful? How can you study the life and teachings of Jesus for forty-two years and still be so critical and vicious?* Then I realized I was dealing with a Teflon mind. The lessons went in one ear and out the other—like that omelet in that skillet they just swirled a bit and then slid off the other side.

Now, put that over against this: a few years ago, a dear friend of ours died. She was in her eighties. I went to the home to visit with the family about the funeral arrangements. As I sat in the den with her four sons, we began to reminisce about their mother. We recalled her best qualities. They mentioned her kindness, her patience, her creativity, her sense of humor, her love for family and the church. Then something very interesting happened. The youngest son said, "Well, I hate to be so blunt, but I loved Mom so much because I was obviously her favorite." "No, you weren't," said another brother. "I was!" Still another brother said, "I always thought I was her favorite." The fourth son said the same. And round and round they went, as only brothers can do, energetically debating about which one was their mother's favorite son. Finally, one of them said: "Jim, that was indeed Mom's greatness. She was so loving that she made not only us but everyone she met feel special!"

That was a beautiful moment. As he said that, I thought of a gospel song—"There's a sweet, sweet Spirit in this place, and I know that it's the Spirit of the Lord." You see, she got that spirit of love from our Lord, who was so adept at making people feel special. The spirit of Christlike love, the spirit of generosity and commitment. We dare not miss those. We must catch the pass and come on home to commitment to God and to all of God's children.

✛ ✛

CHAPTER 4

Come on Home to the Christian Lifestyle

Scripture: Hebrews 12:1-2

The world-famous evangelist Billy Graham tells of the time he was on an airplane when the man in front of him drank too much. The man became loud and rude and ugly to the flight attendant. The more he drank, the worse it got. He became so obnoxious and so obscene and so profane that it was embarrassing to everyone around him. Finally, the flight attendant, trying her best to calm him down, said to him: "Sir, you are being so vulgar and it's embarrassing us because Dr. Billy Graham is seated right behind you." The man turned in his seat, stuck out his hand, and said: "I am so glad to meet you, Dr. Graham. I was at one of your crusades not long ago, and it changed my life!"

Obviously, there is something wrong with that picture. The man had made a vague nod in God's direction, but there was not much commitment there to the Christian lifestyle—and that is so sad. For you see, Christianity is not just a way of believing; it is also a way of behaving. Our faith is not just something we proclaim and celebrate in the sanctuary; it is something we live out and demonstrate and share with others—at home, in the office, on the street, on the tennis court, on a date, and yes, on an airplane.

That man on the airplane reminds me of the old story about the man who had just gotten out of jail. He came back to his home church and when "testimony-time" came, he stood to speak. In a very pious tone, he said, "My friends, it is true that I have mistreated my wife, neglected my children, robbed my neighbors; I have cheated my friends, participated in numerous drunken brawls, broken the law repeatedly, and spent several terms in jail. But I want you to know that in all that time I never once lost my religion!"

The point is clear: talking a good game is not enough. Unless our creeds become deeds, they are not worth much. If we don't practice what we preach, we hurt the cause rather than help it. R. L. Sharpe put it like this:

> Isn't it strange that princes and kings
> And clowns that caper in sawdust rings,

And common folks like you and me
Are builders for eternity.

To each is given a book of rules,
A block of stone and a bag of tools,
And each must shape, ere time has flown,
A stumbling block or a stepping-stone.

As Christians, we are called to be stepping-stones—to join that great cloud of witnesses described in the book of Hebrews (Hebrews 12:1-2). Remember how it reads:

Therefore, since we are surrounded by so great a cloud of witnesses, let us also lay aside every weight and the sin that clings so closely, and let us run with perseverance the race that is set before us, looking to Jesus the pioneer and perfecter of our faith, who for the sake of the joy that was set before him endured the cross, disregarding its shame, and has taken his seat at the right hand of the throne of God.

This means that we are called to be witnesses for Jesus Christ, to commit ourselves to him heart and soul, to live our lives for him, to carry his light of love out to a dark and desperate world.

Have you heard the story about two farmers who lived near each other? One farmer showed up at his neighbor's door one day and said, "Could you please come help me? My son fell into a mudhole and he's stuck." "How deep is he in?" the neighbor asked. "He's up to his ankles!" answered the farmer. "Well, then," said the neighbor, "it's not so bad. We have time for a cup of coffee before we go help him." "I don't think so," said the farmer. "He's in head first!"

Our world is like that today, isn't it? We are stuck in the muck and mire and the mud up to our ankles—and we are in head first! We need somebody to come and save us. We need somebody to deliver us from the dirt and the filth. We need somebody to light a candle and lead us out of the darkness. This is what is so great about the church. We have the one who can save us. We have Jesus Christ. The world is starving to death for Jesus Christ and we have him. Our job is to share him with a needy world.

Now, hold on to your seats, because I'm going to tell you something that may sound very strange. Are you ready? Here it is: We are called to be saints. Now, before you break into a cold sweat, let me hurry to define the term. A saint is one who is so devoted to Christ that he or she makes goodness attractive. A saint is a person who has a radiant, contagious, winsome commitment to God. In Sunday school one Sunday morning, the fourth-grade teacher asked the students this question: "What is a saint?" There was a long pause, and then one little girl remembered the church's stained-glass windows and she said, "A saint is a person the light shines through."

Some time ago, I ran across what could be a formula for becoming a saint. It read like this: "You take an ordinary person, introduce them to Jesus Christ, and then turn them loose on the world for Christ's sake." This passage of Scripture in Hebrews 12 is calling us to be this kind of saint: Join the cloud of witnesses. Lay aside every weight or distraction. Run the race with perseverance. Let the light of Christ shine through you.

Let me be more specific. Let me break this down a bit and list some "saintly qualities" that I have seen in people who have been saints to me, saintly qualities that are especially radiant, attractive, appealing, contagious, and winsome.

⚜ ⚜ ⚜ ⚜ ⚜

FIRST OF ALL, I'VE NOTICED THAT REAL SAINTS HAVE A SENSE OF DIRECTION

They know who they are, where they are going, and who is with them. They are moving toward Christ, not away from him.

There is a wonderful story about the great scientist, Albert Einstein. Einstein was on a train one day that was moving out of New York City. As the conductor came through the passenger coaches, Dr. Einstein began to look frantically through his coat pockets for his ticket. By the time the conductor arrived at where Einstein was seated, the renowned scientist had pulled out all of his pockets in both his trousers and coat, and was proceeding to search through his briefcase.

The conductor immediately recognized Einstein and said: "Please don't worry, Dr. Einstein. I trust you"; and he proceeded to collect the tickets from the rest of the passengers. After about thirty minutes, the conductor walked back through the car where Einstein was located. By this time, Albert Einstein was down on his hands and knees, crawling around the train car, looking and feeling under the seats even more frantically for his ticket. The conductor tried to reassure him: "Dr. Einstein, please don't worry about finding your ticket anymore. It's OK. Just forget it. I trust you." To this, Albert Einstein turned his head upward from his position on the floor and said, "Young man, this is not an issue of trust. It is an issue of direction. I have no idea where I am going."

Isn't this a parable for so many people today? They are on the move, but they have no sense of direction; they are lost and confused and they are frantically looking for some clue because they don't know where they are going.

His name was Jack. He was a coal miner's son. He tells about a terrifying incident that occurred down in the mine when he was a boy. He was in the mine shaft with his father and other miners when something went wrong. The miners had to find their way out of the mine a different way, an unfamiliar way. They struggled through a labyrinth of old workings and stagnant ponds. Jack's father, one of the best miners and a devoted parent, put Jack on his back and led his fellow miners over dangerous ground.

In the foul air, the flames of their open lamps began to weaken. With Jack clutching to the neck of his father, they walked through murky waters that came up to his father's chest. Once out of the water, they started up a steep incline. After they had climbed for a time, Jack's father suddenly pointed upward and said, "Look, Son, look!" Jack said that there seemed to be a bright disk, about the size of a half dollar, on what appeared to be a distant mountain. Jack's dad then said, "Look at that! Isn't that beautiful? That's what we've been looking for, Son, the light of the world. Come on! Let's move toward it!"

Jack said that the light grew in size as they approached it and finally they came out of the darkness into the light of safety on the world's surface. The real saints are those who are moving toward the light. Let me ask you something: do you have a sense of direction? Do you know where you are going? Which way are you moving right now? Toward the light or away from it? The Christian life is a journey, and the question for us today is this: which way are we moving? Are we moving toward Christ or away from him? We can't stand still on this race track. We are constantly moving one way or the other.

Every action, every thought, every word, every decision we make moves us one way or the other. Toward the light or toward the darkness; toward Christ or away from him. This is what Hebrews 12 is all about. Here the Scripture says to us: Run the race with perseverance looking toward Jesus; in other words, run toward him, lay aside every distraction, move toward Jesus. Let that be your sense of direction.

❧ ❧ ❧ ❧ ❧

SECOND, I'VE NOTICED THAT SAINTS HAVE A SENSE OF LOVE

Remember the old song "Precious Memories, How They Linger"? Let me tell you about a precious memory I made some years ago. A good friend called me in tears. His mother had died. She had lived a long, wonderful life and had died in her sleep. I went to the home to try to help the family in their grief and to help plan the funeral. Immediately they said, "Jim, in the service would you read the love chapter (1 Corinthians 13)? It so beautifully summarizes her life. She was always so kind and loving toward everyone." Then they told me about something beautiful she had done over the years. She loved long-stemmed red roses and every time she heard of someone experiencing a joy or a sorrow, she would send them a long-stemmed red rose with a love note.

She used these roses to include people in the circle of her love. Whether it was a birth, a marriage, a graduation, an illness, a disappointment, or a heartache, she would express her love with a red rose. The family, of course, wanted a spray of long-stemmed red roses on her casket. The burial was to be private (for family only), so I suggested to them that after the service they might want to give each member of the family one of those roses from the casket spray to remember Grandma by. They thought that was a good idea.

While we were talking about all of this, the seven-year-old grandson, Charlie, was sitting there fidgeting like any seven-year-old boy would do in that situation. All of this was awkward and heavy and boring to him. He kept stretching and squirming and yawning and wiggling and moaning like little boys are wired up to do. And I remember wishing they would let him go outside and play. I thought to myself, *Bless his heart! He is not into this; he is not listening; he is not interested at all.*

I found out the next day how wrong I was. When the service at the cemetery was over, I stepped out from under the tent and walked over to stand under a shade tree to give them some family time. One by one the family walked by the casket and selected a long-stemmed rose and then returned to their seats. When they were all seated again, the seven-year-old grandson, Charlie, went back to the casket. He was jumping up trying to reach another rose. His dad went over to see what in the world he was doing. Charlie whispered something in his dad's ear. The dad smiled, nodded, and then held Charlie up so he could select another rose. When he put him back down, an amazing thing happened: seven-year-old Charlie walked out of the tent over to the tree where I was standing and handed the rose to me. With that simple act of thoughtfulness, he had caught the spirit of his grandmother and the Christ she served, and he had included me in the family. I didn't think Charlie was listening, but he got the point better than anybody, including his minister. Just like his grandmother would have done, he included me in the circle of love. That was a saintly thing to do, because real saints have a sense of direction and they have a sense of love.

❧ ❧ ❧ ❧ ❧

THIRD, AND FINALLY, REAL SAINTS HAVE A SENSE OF COMMITMENT

Her name was Brittany. She was eleven years old. In January, she began having severe headaches. In April, the diagnosis came in: a malignant brain tumor. Brittany (with great strength and spiritual poise) went through radiation treatments, chemotherapy, and six brain surgeries. Then on a Thursday at 4:00 a.m., she died.

Brittany kept a daily journal, and in her journal she wrote about her battle with cancer. When you read this, you are just amazed by her faith, her hope, her love, and her courage and childlike candor. She writes about her family, her friends, her doctors and nurses, and her pets. She tells about her surgeries and showing her classmates her scar and how someone from the hospital came to her school to do a program on cancer, so the children in her class would not be afraid to be around her or touch her.

She tells about how much she loves pop singer Gloria Estefan and how the Make-a-Wish Foundation made it possible for her to go to Miami to meet Gloria Estefan. She tells about losing her hair, but then says it's OK because she can get a wig like Gloria Estefan's hair. She writes with beautiful, childlike honesty and deep faith, and through it all she never wavers in her commitment to God.

Let me share one excerpt. She writes about going to the funeral of her great-grandmother, G.G., and here's what she says:

> The funeral was OK, but I really wanted to cry, but I didn't because Lynnsey was sitting next to me and I didn't want to upset her. I brought Daisy Ann, my doll, the one G.G. liked so much that I got for Christmas from Mom & Dad.... We looked at G.G. and she looked very pretty ... sort-of-like she was sleeping.... She really isn't there.... It's just her shell that she used on earth. I'm glad that she isn't in pain anymore ... and I'm so glad that we have such a good Heavenly Father to take care of her. I think by now she has wings like an angel.

And I think by now Brittany does, too.

Let me ask you something: do you have faith like that? Do you trust God like that? Are you that committed? That's what makes the saints, saints. They have a sense of direction, a sense of love, and a deep, deep sense of commitment to God.

❧ ❧

CHAPTER 5

Come on Home to the Atmosphere of Christ

Scripture: Romans 12:1-8

Not long ago, a television newsman was interviewing a group of astronauts about the opportunities and dangers of travel in space. He concluded the interview by asking this question: "What do you think is the single most important key to successful space travel?" One of the astronauts made an interesting response. He said, "The

41

secret of traveling in space is to take your own atmosphere with you." As I heard that, I realized that it's also true in our travels through life on this earth. The key is to take your own atmosphere with you. We don't have to be changed or altered or influenced or destroyed by alien or even hostile environments in this life. We can take our own atmosphere with us. That is precisely what this magnificent passage in Paul's Letter to the Romans is about. Paul says, "I appeal to you therefore, . . . by the mercies of God, to present your bodies as a living sacrifice, holy and acceptable to God, which is your spiritual worship. Do not be conformed to this world, but be transformed by the renewing of your minds, so that you may discern what is the will of God—what is good and acceptable and perfect" (Romans 12:1-2).

I like the way J. B. Phillips translates the last part: "Don't let the world around you squeeze you into its own mould" (12:2 Phillips). In other words: "Give your life totally to God and don't let anything change that or water that down or choke the life out of that." Or, put another way: "You can take your own atmosphere with you."

With this in mind, let's break it down a bit and see how it applies to you and me today. What are some of the things we need to take along with us as we journey through this life?

❧ ❧ ❧ ❧ ❧

FIRST, THERE IS COMMITMENT TO GOD

That is an atmosphere we can always take with us wherever we may go; that is really what Romans 12 is all about. What Paul is talking about here is total commitment—unflinching, unswerving, unwavering, unshakeable commitment to God, a complete and absolute dedication to God's righteousness that will not be altered or weakened by any outer circumstances, environments, or influence.

A young husband and wife were trying to make a difficult ethical decision in the business world. They had a chance to make a lot of money on a business deal, only it was a little shady, just a little in the gray area. The offer that had been presented to them was not illegal, but it meant that they would get rich at the expense of other people who were down on their luck. The young man, thinking out loud, said to his wife: "It's the chance of a lifetime. We would be fixed financially forever; but somehow it bothers me, and I find myself hesitating, yet it would give us the security we have wanted."

Suddenly, his wife interrupted: "Tom, we can't do it. We cannot do it."

"Why?" he asked.

"Because," she said, "because of God."

He went to her, they held each other tightly, they cried together, and then he said, "Of course, you're right; you're right."

Now, that is the atmosphere of commitment to God, and wherever we go, we need to take that along with us.

※ ※ ※ ※ ※

SECOND, THERE IS TRUST IN GOD

Several years ago, I conducted a funeral service for one of the finest human beings I have ever known. She died at the age of eighty-seven, the victim of cancer. Whoever coined the word *lady* must have had some-one like her in mind because she was the epitome of what a lady should be—wholesome, bright, kind, thoughtful, tender, gracious, humble, gen-tle. But at the same time, she had a strength of character that was firm, solid, and amazing. I think her spiritual strength came from her tena-cious trust in God, an unflinching trust in God that never wavered.

When the bad news about her malignancy came, I went to try to min-ister to her—and she ministered to me. I was inspired by her strong response to the alien environment of terminal illness. When I saw her there in that hospital room, she looked so fragile and yet radiant. I wanted to be strong for her, but my eyes misted over and my voice choked away to nothing. She reached out and took my hand and said: "Jim, it's OK. I have been so blessed, God has always been with me, and I feel his presence now as never before. When death comes, he will be there for me too. I trust him: I trust him." She had walked into a strange, hostile environment, but she had taken her own atmosphere with her— the atmosphere of commitment to God and the atmosphere of trust in God.

❦ ❦ ❦ ❦ ❦

THIRD, AND FINALLY, THERE IS LOVE FOR GOD

Some years ago, one of our bishops came to speak at a banquet at our church. I met his plane that afternoon and brought him to the church. As we came into the south foyer, one of our young people (who was working at the church for the summer) was down on his hands and knees on the floor, scraping up floor wax. I introduced them and the bishop reached out to shake hands, but the young man said, "Oh, Bishop, you don't want to touch me right now, I've been at this all day and my hands are covered with dirt, grime, and old wax." Undaunted, the bishop smiled and said, "I could use some of that on mine." And then he shook the young man's hand warmly.

The bishop gave a great message at the banquet that night, but you know I don't remember one word of what he said. However, I will never forget that little act of love and kindness in the south foyer: the bishop reaching out to shake the grimy hand of a hardworking teenager. That stuck with me.

Love for others is so important. It's the best way to show our love for God. If you want to please God, if you want to do good for God's kingdom, if you want to bless the church, if you want to continue the ministry of Jesus Christ in this world, then become a loving person. Let God's love flow through you to others.

Wherever you may go, take the atmosphere of love with you; take commitment to God that will not waver; take along trust in God that will not flinch; and take love for God and others. That's what it's all about. That's also what being at home with God is all about.

✤ ✤

CHAPTER 6

Come on Home to Christ's Healing

Scripture: Luke 13:10-17

Some years ago, our son Jeff and I went to a fast-food restaurant to pick up some hamburgers. After placing our order and receiving the food, we walked out of the restaurant to the parking lot. As we got into the car, my back went out. I was bent double. I couldn't straighten up at all and I was in terrific pain. It hurt to move. It hurt to laugh. It hurt to breathe. I was in agony. If you happen to be one of those unfortunate people who suffer from back trouble, you know precisely what I'm talking about.

Jeff drove us home. Then it took him fifteen minutes to get me out of the car and to the front door, a painful pilgrimage of approximately twelve or thirteen yards. When we finally navigated the distance from the car to the front door of our house, I was hurting so badly that I literally could not lift my foot over the threshold. So Jeff turned me sideways and (bent double as I was) he gently toppled me into the house.

I was half in and half out of the door, lying across the threshold. My upper body was inside the house, but my legs were still outside. So, Jeff had to take hold of my feet, lift them high into the air, turn me on to my back, take hold of my ankles, and drag me in.

As he was doing this, we heard a car horn honking. Some of our neighbors were driving by just at that moment, just in time to see Jeff dragging me in the front door by my feet. Well, you can imagine the rumors that began to fly around the neighborhood. Ever since that moment, I have had profound sympathy for people who suffer with back problems.

This fascinating story in Luke 13 is about a woman with a serious back problem. The story doesn't provide many details. Was it arthritis? Or curvature of the spine? Or a muscle problem? Was it caused by old age? Or was it the consequence of a back injury that had not healed properly? Was she bent double by embarrassment? Had something happened years before that bent her over in shame? We just don't know.

The writer does tell us that she had suffered for eighteen years and that she was "bent over and was quite unable to stand up straight" (Luke

13:11). I suppose that after eighteen years, it had become an accepted way of life for her. Her neighbors were accustomed to seeing her like that, making her painful way down the street. You could recognize her from a distance. She was the crooked woman and she had walked a lot of crooked miles in those eighteen years.

Jesus noticed her in the synagogue. Nobody else paid her any mind. She had been a part of the landscape for so long they took her and her "bent-double situation" for granted. It was a Sabbath day, and according to their custom the people had gathered. The men and boys had the places of prominence in those days. The women were restricted to the back of the room. It was a poor vantage point—especially for someone bent double—to see and hear what was going on. Maybe she preferred it that way. Even after eighteen long years you can still be self-conscious about a handicap or disability. Obviously, she was not one of the principal participants in the service. She was just one of those faithful souls who ask only to be allowed to be present.

Jesus saw her. How perceptive he was! So quickly his eyes could find the loneliest and neediest person in the crowd. The room could have been filled to capacity with men of great stature, but still he would have seen this crooked little woman, half hidden by the others. With love, compassion, power, and authority, he called out to her, "You are free of your trouble; you have been all bent out of shape long enough. It's time to straighten up. It's time to stand tall!"

Then he touched her gently—a touch of love, a touch of encouragement, a touch of healing—and immediately she straightened up and began to praise God. When he told her to straighten up, it was a shock but she did it! She didn't stop to argue or debate or ask whether she could. She simply responded to what he said. I can't explain what happened there, but she was healed, she was made whole, she stood up straight, and her crooked days were over.

And they all lived happily ever after. End of story? No! Not quite! It would have been nice if everyone in the synagogue had cheered and run over to congratulate her; but no, as so often happens, there was someone there to strike a sour note. In this case, the spoilsport was none other than the leader of the synagogue. He was a man who took himself very seriously and he saw himself as the watchdog of the rules. He wanted to be sure that all the "t's" were crossed and all the "i's" dotted. There were rules, and he felt obliged to remind people about those rules.

Luke 13 says that he was "indignant" because Jesus had healed on the Sabbath. "Now see here," the leader of the synagogue said, "there are six days to be healed. If you want to be healed, come on those days, not on the Sabbath; it's against the rules to get healed on the Sabbath." Jesus responded. He called that hypocrisy. He pointed out that even devout folks take care of their livestock on the Sabbath. Why not heal this hurting woman? Eighteen years is long enough to be bent double. She shouldn't have to wait another day.

This is a great story, isn't it? It has everything: suffering and healing, laws and grace, bad news and good news, pride and humility, legalism and love, problems and solutions. I want us to think together about this story because there are so many ways today that people can get all bent out of shape. We get our backs slumped over; we can get bent double with guilt and anxiety, with fears and worries, with burdens and responsibilities. Let me show you what I mean.

✤ ✤ ✤ ✤ ✤

FIRST, WE CAN GET ALL BENT OUT OF SHAPE AS A NATION

That's right. Whole nations can get bent double. History has shown that dramatically. In my opinion, America is the greatest nation on the face of the earth, the greatest nation in all of history; but we are presently confronting the single most dangerous problem we have ever faced, a problem that is bending us to the breaking point. We are facing an evil so insidious and so destructive that it is threatening to tear our nation and indeed our world apart.

I'm talking about the drug problem. I'm talking about drug abuse. Illegal drugs are bending us, as a nation, all out of shape. Did you know that 85 percent of the crime in the United States today is drug related? Eighty-five percent! Did you know that the cost to our nation for this drug crisis is estimated at 300 billion dollars a year? Not even to mention what it costs us in human lives.

Did you know that the average age for the first-time drug user in America is now eleven years old? Did you know that our nation now has the largest demand for and consumption of illegal drugs on the face of the earth? And did you know that "all that's necessary for the triumph of evil is for good people to do nothing"? The drug problem is bending us double as a nation, and if our Lord could speak to us today, I know (without question) he would say to us, "Straighten up! Straighten up! This has gone on long enough!" He would say to us, "Say no to drugs and yes to faith."

Some years ago, there was a big sign on a vacant lot in Atlanta, Georgia, that read: "Future Home of Avondale Christian Church . . . God Willing." Someone came along later and wrote these words underneath: "God Is Willing! Are You?" We, as a nation, can whip the drug problem if we are willing, if we want to, if we take it on. If we, as a nation, make up our mind to stop it, with the help of God, we can. But we need to stand up now. We need to stand tall now. As a nation we need to stiffen our backbones now.

❧ ❧ ❧ ❧ ❧

SECOND, WE CAN GET ALL BENT OUT OF SHAPE AS FAMILIES

A few weeks ago, I went to another city to participate in a wedding in a large and beautiful Episcopal church. The Episcopal priest, whose first name is Nathan, welcomed me warmly and graciously. He is an outstanding young man, talented, bright, capable, and committed. I enjoyed him very much. He has a delightful wife and two beautiful young children. As we worked together to get ready to perform the wedding, he told me his story.

He had not always been an Episcopalian. Actually, he had grown up in another religion, another faith altogether. But then he went to college at an Episcopal school. While there, he had a dramatic conversion experience—a conversion experience so powerful that he not only became a Christian but also felt the call to become an Episcopal priest.

However, when Nathan went home and told his parents, they kicked him out of the house. They purged the house of all his personal belongings. They tore all of his pictures out of the family photo albums. His father said to him: "You are dead to us! You never existed!" This happened some years ago, and to this day, his father and mother, his sisters and brothers refuse to speak to him. They will not look at him. They refuse to acknowledge his existence.

Last summer, a distant cousin hosted a family reunion, and he attempted reconciliation by inviting Nathan to come. Nathan went, but (except for the host) no one spoke to him; no one looked at him. He would walk up to a group of relatives and they would pretend that he was not there. They shunned him totally. "How do you handle that, Nathan?" I asked him. "Well," he said, "it's been very difficult, and recently it's been tough because our children have reached the age where they are asking: 'Where are our grandparents? Why don't they ever come to visit us? Why can't we go see them?'" Isn't that sad? Just think what those grandparents are missing.

If our Lord could speak to families that get all bent out of shape like that, you know he would say: "Straighten up! Stand tall! You've hurt long enough! Rise above it!"

❧ ❧ ❧ ❧ ❧

THIRD, AND FINALLY, WE CAN GET ALL BENT OUT OF SHAPE AS PERSONS

Life with its heavy burdens and difficult problems can twist and pummel us as individuals and rip into us like a Mike Tyson left hook. Life with its hard knocks can take the wind out of our sails. But, faith in Christ can enable us to stand tall. Faith in Christ can give us the spiritual backbone to stand firm when times are tough. Faith in Christ can give us the confidence and strength to press on when troubles and burdens weigh down so heavily upon us.

Just recently, a good friend brought me a poem called "The Roses of Life" that says it well. Listen to this:

> I've dreamed many dreams that never came true
> I've seen them vanish at dawn,
> But I've realized enough of my dreams, thank God,
> To make me want to dream on.
>
> I've prayed many prayers when my answer never came
> Though I waited patient and long,
> But answers have come to enough of my prayers
> To keep me praying on.
>
> I've trusted many a friend who failed,
> And left me to weep alone,
> But I've found enough of my friends true blue,
> To keep me trusting on.
>
> I've sown many seeds that fell by the way
> For the birds to feed upon,
> But I've held enough golden sheaves in my hands
> To keep me sowing on.
>
> I've drained the cup of disappointment and pain,
> And gone many days without song,

But I've sipped enough nectar from the roses of life
To make me want to live on.

I've been way down many times in my life,
Knocked flat by the stresses that fall,
But God's always there to lift me again,
To help me keep standing tall!

When we feel all bent out of shape, when we feel pressed down and burdened, when we feel bent double, Christ is there for us with his special brand of healing, saying: "Straighten up! Stand up! Rise above it! Stand tall!"

❧ ❧

CHAPTER 7

Come on Home to Servanthood

Scripture: Luke 22:24-27

There is no question about it. As Christians we are "Called to Be Servants." We, as Christian people, are called of God, not to be dignitaries, not to be royalty, not to be aristocrats, but to be servants, God's servant people. It's so important to remember that because the great temptation of the church is now, and always has been, to think of ourselves as privileged people rather than servant people; to think of ourselves as God's special favorites rather than as God's humble servants. And when we give in to that temptation and begin to think of our rights, our high place, our benefits, our special consideration, our privileges—at that point we depart from the spirit of Christ and fail to be God's church.

The culprit word that gets us into trouble goes all the way back to the Old Testament. It's the word *chosen* as in "God's chosen people." *Chosen*: it's a good word gone bad. To us, *chosen* means "choice," "select," "better than," "holier," "privileged," "deserving of preferential treatment." But that's not what God had in mind at all. We are chosen not for privilege, but for service. We are chosen not to sit in high places, but to do hard work. We are chosen not because we are good, but because God is good. We are chosen not to royally occupy some elegant spot of honor, but to be God's humble servants to a needy world. We are chosen not to have the red carpet rolled out to us, but rather to roll up our sleeves and to get busy with God's work of redeeming this broken world. Listen! If every member of the church understood that we are called to be servants—not privileged people, but servants—if we all understood that and embraced that and practiced that, we could turn this world upside down for God. If every member of the church saw herself or himself as God's committed humble servant, 90 percent of our problems would be solved. We would have no staffing problems, no money problems, no burn-out problems, no drop-out problems. No one would ever get offended or get their feelings hurt. No one would ever be difficult, or resentful, or jealous, or petty, or selfish.

In 1935, Albert Schweitzer spoke to a graduating class at an English boys' school. He said: "I don't know what your destiny will be. Some of you will perhaps occupy remarkable positions. Perhaps some of you will become famous by your pens or as artists. But I know one thing: the only ones among you who will be really happy are those who have sought and found how to serve." Those words are so true. You can mark them down. Service is indeed the key to happiness because it is the call of God.

But sometimes we forget, don't we? We forget that we are called to be humble servants, and that is precisely when we get off track. We see a sad example of this in the Scripture lesson for today in Luke 22, where the disciples get into a hostile, jealous dispute about (of all things) "which one of them is the greatest." Can you imagine? Can you picture that? I mean, this sounds like something you would see on a TV promo for world-class wrestling. We can easily picture Hulk Hogan, Macho Man, and One Man Gang screaming at one another about which one of them is the greatest, but the disciples? The disciples? And that's not the worst of it. Look where it's happening—in the Upper Room, at the Lord's Table, during Holy Communion!

Here's how the New English Bible records it.

> [The disciples had just received the bread and wine when] a jealous dispute broke out: who among them should rank highest? But [Jesus] said: "In the world, kings lord it over their subjects.... Not so with you: on the contrary, the highest among you must bear himself like the youngest, the chief of you like a servant. For who is greater— the one who sits at table or the servant who waits on him? Surely the

one who sits at table. Yet here am I among you like a servant." (Luke 22:24-27 NEB)

The disciples had a hard time grasping that "servant" concept. Jesus had to go to the cross and rise from the dead to get their attention. In a backdoor way, we learn from the disciples here how not to come into the presence of God.

✤ ✤ ✤ ✤ ✤

FIRST, IT'S CLEAR THAT WE DON'T COME IN THE SPIRIT OF ARROGANCE

Arrogantly, the disciples squabbled at the Lord's Table about which of them was the greatest. Jesus had to step in and say: Have I been so long with you? Don't you get it? Don't you understand? Don't you see how I'm being a servant? I washed your feet, I served the bread. Can't you see that I'm trying to teach you how to be servants?

Some years ago, a celebrity here in America was asked if he believed in God. His answer was the epitome of arrogance. He said: "Of course I believe in God. We are good buddies. When I get to heaven, I'm going to play golf every day. In fact, I'm going to ask Jesus to play golf with me, and if he doesn't like to play, I'll let him be my caddy."

There is no place for that kind of arrogance at the Lord's Table or in the Christian's heart. We can't come into the presence of God with that kind of arrogant attitude.

❧ ❧ ❧ ❧ ❧

SECOND, IT'S ALSO CLEAR THAT WE DON'T COME IN THE SPIRIT OF HOSTILITY

As we read Luke 22, we see the disciples turning what should have been a love-feast into a battleground for their hostilities. Hatefully, they attack one another and dispute with one another until Jesus steps in and calls them back to their senses.

Famous football coach Lou Holtz is noted for his sense of humor, as well as for winning football games. At an annual sales meeting of the Western Insurance Companies, he told about a man driving home from a party one night when a policeman pulled him over. The policeman said: "Sir, were you in a hurry? You were driving seventy-seven miles per hour." The man turned hostile. "You're crazy. I wasn't driving anywhere near that fast. I had it on cruise control. I was driving fifty-five!" "Sorry, sir," said the policeman, "my radar clocked you at seventy-seven." The man said, "You are stupid and incompetent. I'm going to report you to the mayor and the police chief. I'm going to have your job and your badge, and then I'm going to punch you in the nose!" Patiently, the policeman turned to the man's wife and said, "Is he always like this?" The wife replied, "Only when he's drunk!"

Somehow, I don't think that helped the situation! Some folk don't have to get drunk to get hostile. Some folk seem to have been born in the objective mood. But there's no place for arrogance or hostility at the Lord's Table or in the Christian's heart. We can't come into the presence of God with arrogance and hostility tainting our souls.

❧ ❧ ❧ ❧ ❧

THIRD, IT'S ALSO CLEAR FROM LUKE 22 THAT WE DON'T COME IN THE SPIRIT OF RESENTMENT

Resentment, jealousy, envy, selfishness—whatever label you want to put on it, there was a lot of that brewing in the group of disciples that evening in the Upper Room. Each disciple was saying in his own way, "I'm going to get ahead no matter who I have to step on or push aside. If I have to elbow other people out of the way, then so be it." It's not a very pretty picture, is it? This is a sad moment to me; there is great pathos about this. The disciples have, for some time now, heard Jesus teach and preach. They have seen him live, they have felt his love; but they don't get it. They are still thinking about preferential treatment. They are still caught up in selfish interests and ruthless ambition.

We know, of course, that later they came around; finally the lightbulb turned on for them and they caught the spirit. But here in Luke 22, they are still mixed up, and for a moment their communion turns "unholy."

What's the message for us here? Simply this, we come to the Lord's Table and to life, not in arrogance, not in hostility, not in resentment, but in humility and love, as God's servants.

I think the truth of it all is wrapped up in a beautiful story Bishop Will Willimon told some years ago in *The Christian Ministry* magazine (*The Christian Ministry*, July-August, 1989, p. 47).

It was a cold Christmas Eve a few years ago and my family was running late for the Communion service. Where are my sermon notes? Who has my collar? Don't forget to turn the lights off. Everybody get in the car and keep quiet. On the way to the church, my five-year-old daughter, Harriet, who had been looking rather pale all day, finally got sick, throwing up in the car. Great, I thought. If people only knew what preachers go through.

I wheeled into the church parking lot and jumped out of the car, leaving my wife, Patsy, to clean up the car and get the kids into church. If people only knew what preachers' spouses go through. Patsy led a still unsteady and pale Harriet into the church, suggesting that they sit on the back pew, in the darkness, in case she got sick again. Our son, William, aged seven, ran down to the front of the church to join his visiting grandparents.

I hastily threw on my robe, took a deep breath, and joined the choir for the processional. I made it through the first part of the service and the sermon. Then came the Eucharist. I prayed, broke the bread, poured the wine and invited everyone forward for communion. Patsy said it never occurred to her to suggest that Harriet go forward to receive Communion. After all she wasn't feeling good, despite its being the night before Christmas. Patsy went down, then returned to her seat in the darkened rear of the church.

She noticed seven-year-old William got up from where he was sitting and went back to the communion rail (for the second time). What was he up to? She watched him race to the back of the church . . . scoot down the pew toward his little sister. He opened his hands, revealing a small piece of bread. "Harriet," he said, "the body of Christ, given for you." Without hesitating, she picked the bread out of his hands and plopped it into her mouth saying, "Amen." Then young William scooted back down the pew and ran back to join his grandparents.

I don't mean to be sentimental or gushy ... but I want to ponder the significance of the fact that, when God chose to come among us, God chose to come as a child.

That's how we come to the Lord's Table and to life; that's how we are to live every day—not in arrogance, not in hostility, not in resentment, but as a loving, thoughtful child of God, and as a humble, faithful servant.

❧ ❧

CHAPTER 8

Come on Home to the Spirit of Gratitude

Scripture: Luke 19:1-10

Have you heard about the sales manager of a large corporation who was complaining to his secretary one day about one of his workers? "That Harry is a real loser. He is so inept. He has no talent at all! He can't do anything right. I asked him to pick up a newspaper on his way back from lunch, but I'll bet you anything that he botches it up." Just then, the door burst open. It was Harry, and he had an excited look on his face. "Guess what!" he exclaimed. "You won't believe what happened! Great news! At lunch I ran into Mr. Jones, who hasn't given us an order in seven years. I visited with him about our new line and I talked him into a one-million-dollar contract. Here is his check for a million dollars!" The sales manager sighed rather disgustedly and turned to his secretary. "What did I tell you?" he said. "Just as I thought, he forgot the newspaper."

A lot of people in the world today are just like that sales manager. No matter what kind of wonderful things happen to them, no matter what kind of wonderful situations they find themselves in, they still have a way of spotting what's wrong, focusing on it intently, and harping on it constantly. And the truth is that all of us have our moments of spiritual blindness, moments when we are just unable to see how blessed we are. The riches of life, the riches of God are all around us wherever we are, and yet so often we are unable to see them because we tend to magnify our difficulties, overlook our advantages, and fail to see the good in what we have.

This is why we need thanksgiving. It not only reminds us to give thanks to God for all that we have, but it also reminds us of who we are, to whom we belong, and upon whom we depend. There is a beautiful example of the real spirit of thanksgiving in the New Testament story of Zacchaeus.

In Jesus' encounter with Zacchaeus, we discover a fascinating formula for thanksgiving and how it can dramatically change our lives. Remember the story with me. Jesus and his disciples were going to Jerusalem. Jesus was heading toward the cross. As they came to Jericho, a great crowd gathered to see him. Zacchaeus was in the crowd. The Scripture tells us that he was a "chief tax collector and was rich." Zacchaeus was disliked and despised by the people of Jericho—for a number of reasons.

For one thing, they disliked Zacchaeus because he was the chief tax collector. He was responsible for gathering the hated Roman tax on the products of Jericho, such as balsam, and upon the costly imports from Damascus and Arabia. In the days of Jesus, the tax collectors were known for their greed, were considered outcasts, and classed with thieves and cutthroats. Zacchaeus was a chief tax collector, so he was greatly despised.

Also, Zacchaeus was regarded by the people of Jericho as a "traitor." He was a fellow Jew who had betrayed his people, his nation, his faith, and his God. To them, he was a turncoat who had gotten "rich" at their expense. So, they resented him and rejected him.

This was the setting when Jesus came to Jericho that day. Zacchaeus was eager to see Jesus, but being a little man he could not see over the crowd. He ran ahead and climbed a sycamore tree in the hope of getting a glimpse of the great teacher. When Jesus saw Zacchaeus, he sensed his loneliness and his heart went out to him. Jesus went over, looked up, and said, "Zacchaeus, hurry and come down, for I must stay at your house today." Zacchaeus, overwhelmed by the master's acceptance of him and by this special honor, jumped down quickly and welcomed Jesus, and Zacchaeus's whole life was changed. Christ does that to us. Thanksgiving does that to us. Zacchaeus was so grateful for this acceptance, so filled with thanksgiving that it absolutely turned his life around.

Notice that Jesus gave him no material gifts. He gave him something better—love, respect, and acceptance.

Zacchaeus was so thankful that his lifestyle was totally changed. Why, it even touched his pocketbook. "Behold, Lord," he says, "the half of my goods I give to the poor; and if I have taken any thing from any man by false accusation, I restore him fourfold" (Luke 19:8 KJV). You see, that's what real thanksgiving does—it changes our lives. Let me show you what I mean.

Christ gave Zacchaeus three things: a new appreciation, a new evaluation, and a new motivation. Let's take a look at these special qualities one at a time.

❦ ❦ ❦ ❦ ❦

FIRST, CHRIST GAVE ZACCHAEUS A NEW APPRECIATION

Up to this point, Zacchaeus seems to have been basically selfish, thinking only of himself. His motto was "What's in it for me?" But then Jesus came into his life, and that special love ignited within Zacchaeus the spark of gratitude. You see, there is no such thing as an ungrateful Christian. Christianity is by definition thanksgiving. Why do we come to church? Because we are thankful. Why do we sing our hymns? Because we are thankful. Why do we serve God? Because we are thankful. Why do we love one another? Because we are thankful to God to be part of God's family.

Most of us respond appreciatively to what is unusual or rare. For example, if somebody called us today and told us that we had just inherited twenty million dollars, chances are that we would be appreciative of that. If someone called and told us that we had just won a Mercedes or a trip to Hawaii, we would probably be grateful for it. But please notice that it is Jesus' enthusiasm for the seemingly ordinary and commonplace things that reveals his real appreciative spirit.

Remember Jesus' frequent references to simple things: brooms, candles, leaven, old cloth, and the like. Such things we so easily take for granted, but Jesus saw in them the truths of God, the goodness of God, the blessings of God. He wove them into the very texture of his message. Look also at his appreciation of nature: flowers, birds, seeds, sunsets, the wind, the grass of the fields—all spoke to him of the Creator. Not only that, but who ever so appreciated people? Now, most of us appreciate the great and famous personalities like Schweitzer or Saint Francis or Mother Teresa or Wesley or Paul or Moses. But Jesus saw every person, every single person (even a Zacchaeus), as a child of God; and he appreciated and respected all people as a part of the family. Such was the appreciative spirit of Jesus.

In a hated tax collector, he saw a promising disciple. In the weak and vacillating Simon Peter, he saw a rock. In a cup of cold water, he saw divine compassion. In a lily (the commonest of Palestinian flowers), he saw a glory greater than Solomon's. In a sparrow (the commonest of birds), he saw the providence and watch-care of God. In a grain of mustard seed (the smallest of seeds), he saw the kingdom of heaven. And in the face of a little child, he saw the keys to the kingdom. Zacchaeus caught the spark that day when Christ walked into his life—a new appreciation.

❦ ❦ ❦ ❦ ❦

SECOND, CHRIST GAVE ZACCHAEUS A NEW EVALUATION

Jesus gave Zacchaeus a new set of priorities, a new way of measuring what is really valuable.

There once was a young man who had been a very successful doctor. He was highly regarded and greatly respected in the medical profession in his city and state. He was affluent, with a beautiful home, a gorgeous ranch, a lake house, and a country club membership. He had it all: professional success, financial success, and social success. He had what Madison Avenue would call "the big three": wealth, youth, and power.

But then one day, he walked away from all of that. He left it all to become a medical missionary in a poverty-stricken area on the African continent. He loved his life; but he felt God calling him to another life—the life of service to needy people in a remote corner of the world.

After serving in Africa for some time, he came back home for a brief visit. He was asked to speak at his local church. When he was introduced, his host described in great detail the life he had left behind to become a medical missionary.

As the young man spoke that night, he talked graphically about his work in Africa. He told about sleeping in tents and run-down shacks; he told about eating beans and sausages out of a can; he told about performing surgery in a "makeshift, tent operating room" with a colleague holding a small flashlight to help him see as he performed one surgery after another; he told about working in hot and humid areas where there was no electricity and therefore no air-conditioning or power-operated fans; he told about difficult and sometimes dangerous travel experiences that were necessary to get him to small villages, where without him the people had no access to a doctor; he told about standing on his feet sometimes for sixteen straight hours as the villagers streamed in hour after hour to receive the medical care that he could provide.

The people who heard him that night in his home church were moved, touched, and inspired by his message and his story. One lady shook his hand after his presentation and said, "Oh, Doctor, I am so sorry that you are having such a hard time of it." To which the young doctor said, "You misunderstood me. I am having the time of my life!"

Now, let me hurry to say that there was nothing wrong with the doctor's earlier, successful life. He could have stayed in that situation and served God in remarkable ways as well. But he took up his new life as a medical missionary because he felt God calling him to that ministry. He responded to that call with faith, hope, and love, and in so doing he found a new kind of success.

Jesus' way of evaluating success turns our world upside down. He shows us that a sense of meaning is more important than material wealth, that discipleship is better than dollars, that helping others is more fulfilling than "feathering our own nest." Zacchaeus caught the spark that day and he came down out of that sycamore tree with a new appreciation, a new evaluation.

❧ ❧ ❧ ❧ ❧

THIRD, CHRIST GAVE ZACCHAEUS A NEW MOTIVATION

Zacchaeus got converted from selfishness to self-givingness. Zacchaeus got converted from "that belongs to me" to "I belong to that." If thanksgiving is Recognition of God's Generosity, then Christian living is Imitation of God's Generosity.

In 1985, there was a disastrous earthquake in Mexico City. A few days after the earthquake, a little Japanese-American boy was going door-to-door in Los Angeles selling picture postcards for twenty-five cents each. He was giving the profits to earthquake relief. One man bought some postcards from the little boy and asked the boy how much he hoped to raise. The little boy answered quickly, "One million dollars." The man smiled and said, "Do you mean to tell me that you are trying to raise a million dollars to help the earthquake victims all by yourself?" "Oh no, sir," replied the little boy. "My little brother is helping me!"

When Christ comes into our lives, we can't sit still, we have to take up his ministry of love. That becomes the new motivation. It's expressed powerfully in the New Testament. Remember these words from 1 John 4:

> Beloved, let us love one another, because love is from God; everyone who loves is born of God and knows God. Whoever does not love does not know God, for God is love.... We love because he first loved us. Those who say, "I love God," and hate their brothers or sisters, are

liars; for those who do not love a brother or sister whom they have seen, cannot love God whom they have not seen. (4:7-8, 19-20)

The great Christian, Augustine, in his Homily 5 on 1 John, expressed it strongly like this:

Love alone, then, distinguishes between the children of God and the children of the devil. All may sign themselves with the sign of Christ's cross; all may answer "Amen"; all may be baptized; all may go into the churches; all may construct the walls of basilicas. The children of God are not distinguished from the children of the devil except by charity. Those who have charity have been born of God; those who do not have it have not been born of God.

Christ walked into Zacchaeus's life that day in Jericho long ago and gave him a new appreciation, a new evaluation, and a new motivation. He wants to do that for us today. As he did for Zacchaeus that day long ago in Jericho, Christ wants to do the same for us; he wants to bring us home to oneness with God and oneness with our neighbors.

CHAPTER 9

Come on Home
to Generosity

Scripture: Luke 6:45-49

In his book *A Scent of Love*, Keith Miller tells a funny but true story about a mother who took her children to the Animal Farm. The Animal Farm is a place where you can pet animals that roam free—you can even ride an elephant. Unable to find a conventional parking place, the mother parked their little red Volkswagen Bug on a paved pathway that led away from the ranger station. Then she and the children went out and had a great time with the animals.

Toward the end of the day, the mother realized that time had gotten away and they were supposed to pick up Dad that evening at the airport. She hurriedly gathered the children together and rushed to the parking lot. When they got to the car, they made a startling discovery. In her words, "The front end of the car was just smashed." Furious, she stalked up to the ranger station and banged loudly on the door. Before she could speak, the ranger at the desk said, "Lady, you don't have to say a word. I'll bet I know who you are. You're the owner of the little red Volkswagen Bug." He assured her that the Farm would pay for the car's repair. Then he explained how the damage took place.

It so happened that Millie, the elephant that takes children for rides, was trained in the circus to sit on a little red tub. "When Millie saw your car," the ranger explained, trying to stifle a laugh, "she couldn't resist; she sat on it. But don't worry; we will fix it for you good as new." Fortunately, the motor was in the rear of Volkswagen Beetles of that time, so the car was drivable. Quickly they all jumped in the car, and Mom drove off down the freeway going as fast as she dared. Suddenly she came to a long line of backed-up traffic—there had been a pile-up ahead.

She sat there and waited as patiently as she could, but finally decided that the situation called for unusual and creative measures. She whipped the little red Bug over onto the shoulder and started making her way around the long line of cars. Suddenly, a motorcycle patrolman was behind her with lights flashing and siren screaming. When he pulled her over, he said: "Look, lady, don't you know it is against state law to leave the scene of an accident?" "But officer," she answered, "I haven't been involved in any accident." He raised his eyebrows and looked at the front of her car and asked, "Well, what happened to your car?" She replied, "An elephant sat on it." That's when the officer brought out a little balloon for her to breathe into!

You may want to make me breathe into a little balloon when you realize that in this chapter, I am writing about giving, about stewardship, about generosity.

Actually, this matter of giving was tremendously important to Jesus. Did you know that out of the thirty major parables of Jesus, twenty of them relate to our possessions and our giving? Did you know that in the four Gospels (Matthew, Mark, Luke, and John) one verse out of every seven relates to our attitude toward our material possessions? Obviously, giving is a spiritual matter of eternal significance. It is one of the ways we express our gratitude to God. It is one of the ways we do our part to keep the church alive and well. It is one of the ways we help make this world a better place. It is one of the ways we continue the preaching, teaching, healing, helping, caring ministry of Jesus Christ.

Recently, some American tourists in Spain came upon a poignant statue. It showed Jesus bending over and reaching out to help a child who had fallen. The child is on the ground with skinned knees. He has a look of pain on his face and tears in his eyes. With compassion and concern Jesus is leaning over and reaching out to help, but the statue of Jesus has no hands. The tourists are puzzled. "Has the statue been damaged?" "No," answers the tour guide, "that's the way the artist created this originally." Then, with a warm smile, the guide showed the Americans some words written on the base of the statue. The words were in Spanish, so the guide had to translate. He said, "In English the words mean 'We are now his hands.'"

The artist was making a significant statement, wasn't he? He was reminding us that so often when it comes to giving and helping, we want it to be done, but we really want somebody else to do it. As far as Christ's ministry is concerned, however, there is nobody else to do it. It's on us now. If we want it to get done, we have to do it. If our church is to continue to reach out to others to help and heal, we (with the help of God) have to give it hands. It's our turn, our opportunity, our responsibility, our privilege, and our joy. As Paul put it, God loves a cheerful giver.

Over the years I have noticed that there are three kinds of Christian givers. Let's take a look at these and see if we can find ourselves somewhere between the lines.

✤ ✤ ✤ ✤ ✤

FIRST, THERE ARE GRIOT GIVERS

Are you familiar with the word *griot*? It's a West African word. The noted theologian, Martin Marty, introduced me to the word.

He told of reading an old prayer in a Moravian prayer book. The prayer went like this: "O Lord, help us to be faithful storytellers, narrators, teachers, and griots. Amen." Martin Marty said he was reading the prayer rather casually, but then he stumbled over that word *griot*. He had never heard or seen the word before. Was it a typographical error? Or was it valid? He went to the dictionary. The *Oxford English Dictionary* had no such word. He kept looking and finally found the word in the

American Heritage Dictionary. He read the definition quietly to himself: "Griot—a storyteller in West Africa who perpetuates the oral tradition and history of a village or family." Martin Marty said when he read that, he thought, *A griot is what I want to be when I grow up!* (See the *Christian Century,* M.E.M.O., March 15, 1995, p. 311.)

A griot is one who has dedicated himself or herself to the task of keeping alive and well what is special about the family. A griot giver is one who gives to the church out of a sense of duty and responsibility and love. Griot givers are the people who remember with admiration those who went before us and the great work they did, and now feel a burning sense of obligation to take up the torch, hold it high, and carry it forward.

A little boy said to his mother one day: "Mom, you know that special lamp that you love so much, the one that's been in our family for so many generations. Well, this generation just dropped it!" The griot givers are those who don't want to drop it; they feel a keen sense of responsibility, a sacred obligation to keep the lamp burning so as to honor the past, celebrate the present, and protect and insure the future.

One of my favorite poems is "The Bridge Builder" by Will Allen Dromgoole. It's a beautiful example of griot giving—giving out of a sense of duty and responsibility and love. Listen to these powerful words:

> An old man going on a lone highway,
> Came, at the evening, cold and gray,

To a chasm, vast, and deep, and wide,
Through which was flowing a sullen tide.

The old man crossed in the twilight dim;
The sullen stream had no fear for him;
But he turned, when safe on the other side,
And built a bridge to span the tide.

"Old man," said a fellow pilgrim, near,
"You are wasting strength with building here;
Your journey will end with the ending day;
You never again must pass this way.
You've crossed the chasm, deep and wide,
Why build you this bridge at the evening tide?"

The builder lifted his old gray head:
"Good friend, in the path I have come," he said,
"There followeth after me today,
A youth, whose feet must pass this way.

This chasm, that has been naught for me,
To that fair-haired youth may a pitfall be.
He, too, must cross in the twilight dim;
Good friend, I am building this bridge for him."

That poem reminds me of something I ran across recently that describes the difference between a statesman and a politician: "A statesman thinks of the next generation, while a politician thinks of the next election." Some of the great statesmen of the church are griot givers—and thank God for them!

❧ ❧ ❧ ❧ ❧

SECOND, THERE ARE GRATEFUL GIVERS

These are the cheerful givers that Paul mentions in his First Letter to the Corinthians, those who are so grateful to God for all God has done for them that they give cheerfully, joyously, enthusiastically.

A man walked into a mission hospital one day. He saw a young woman missionary washing the ugly sores on the legs and feet of patients with leprosy, and he said: "I wouldn't do that for $100,000!" The missionary nurse looked up at him; she smiled warmly and said, "Neither would I!"

It's amazing what we can do when we are grateful to God for the many blessings God pours out upon us. When we are truly grateful to God for what God has done for us in Jesus Christ our Lord and Savior, it makes us thanks givers; it makes us grateful givers.

Harold Hyde, the president of New Hampshire's Plymouth State College, may well have given the shortest commencement address in history—just three statements long. Here it is:

"Know yourself," said Socrates.
"Control yourself," said Cicero.
"Give yourself," said Jesus Christ.

First, there are the griot givers—those who give out of a sense of duty and responsibility because they are dedicated to keep the church alive and well. Second, there are the grateful givers—those who give out of a deep spirit of appreciation and thankfulness to God for what God has done for us in Jesus Christ and for what God continues to do for us day in and day out.

✤ ✤ ✤ ✤ ✤

THIRD, AND FINALLY, THERE ARE THE GENEROUS GIVERS

These are the second-mile givers. They do their part and more. They stand tall in our midst, like spiritual giants, not because of the size of their gift but because of the loving, thoughtful, gracious, and generous spirit in which they give it. The generous givers are those who have fallen in love with God and God's church, and they are not in love with their money. They see money as God's gift to us to be used to serve God and God's church, to be used to continue the ministry and sacrificial love of Jesus Christ.

Each year all of us receive numerous requests for financial support of many wonderful organizations, worthy agencies in our community working to help children and youth and the unemployed or the homeless and on and on. I know all about that, I get them too. At this moment, I have nine such requests on my desk and eight more at home. They are all wonderful causes. But would it surprise you if I told you that I believe with all my heart that the church should be at the top of our list? The church should come first because the Bible says so and because the church is already doing all of those things.

I like to think of it like this: the church is the General Practitioner Helping Agency. We make house calls. We do it all. You name it, if it's good, the church is doing it: helping children and youth, singles, families, mature adults; helping the sick and the hurting, the grief-stricken and heartbroken; doing worship, music, counseling, recovery, enrichment, the arts, drama. The church is the general practitioner. We do it all.

But, you know, there is still another reason the church should come first in our giving that is even more important, namely this: we have Jesus Christ—the one thing this world needs most! It is one thing to feed the hungry, or clothe the needy, or visit the sick. It's another thing entirely to do those things in the name of Jesus Christ. The generous givers understand that and embrace that and cherish that.

As Christians, we are called to stand tall now and do our part. We are called to be griot givers, grateful givers, and generous givers.

❧ ❧

Come on Home to the
Good News of Christmas

Scripture: Matthew 2:1-12

An old story tells about a factory that was having a terrible problem
with employee theft. Valuable items were being stolen every day,
and the factory managers simply could not figure out who was doing it
or how it was being done. They just knew that they were suffering significant financial losses because of the persistent stealing, and they knew

that it was an inside job. So they hired a security firm to literally search every employee as he or she left at the end of the day. Most of the workers willingly went along with emptying their pockets and having their lunch boxes checked because they were made to realize how serious the "theft problem" had become. But one man would go through the gate every day at closing time with a wheelbarrow full of trash. The exasperated security guard would have to spend a half-hour or more digging through the food wrappers, the aluminum cans, and the Styrofoam cups to see if anything valuable was being smuggled out. He never found anything. Weeks and weeks went by and he never found anything, but still great losses were being suffered on account of employee theft.

Finally one day, the guard could no longer stand it. So, he said to the man, "Look, I know you're up to something, but every day I check every last bit of trash in the wheelbarrow and never find anything worth stealing. It's driving me crazy. Tell me what you're up to and I promise not to report you." The man shrugged and said, "It's simple. I'm stealing wheelbarrows!"

Sometimes we can't see the forest for the trees. Sometimes we can't see the wheelbarrows for the trash. And sometimes we can't see the gifts Christmas gives to us. Christmas is a time for giving. We all know that's true because every year at Christmas, we get all involved in "making our lists and checking them twice." I want to turn the coin over, go a step deeper, and take a look with you at the gifts Christmas gives to us. Yes, the gifts Christmas gives to us, because without question, they are the most important of all.

Some months ago, our family was invited to a unique birthday party. A close friend asked us to come to his home to celebrate his wife's birthday. Ten or twelve people attended the party, and we were all told rather strongly NOT to bring gifts. "No Gifts Please" the invitation said in bold, capital letters, with two exclamation points. No gifts—they really meant it.

It was a delightful evening—a sumptuous meal, excellent entertainment, good conversation, good fun, and fellowship. Finally, the cake was brought in and we all sang "Happy Birthday." Then something happened at this birthday party that I had never seen before. The man stood up and with a wide smile, he said: "My wife celebrates her birthday in a unique way. Instead of receiving gifts from others, she likes to celebrate her birthday by giving gifts to those she loves." And she proceeded to bring out special gifts for all the people there.

Something like this happens at Christmas. Christmas has some very special gifts for you and me. The Christ Child celebrates his birthday by giving special gifts to those he loves. Let me list for your consideration three very special gifts that Christmas gives us.

A New Picture of God

A New Partnership with Others

A New Purpose for Living

✤ ✤ ✤ ✤ ✤

FIRST, CHRISTMAS GIVES US A NEW PICTURE OF GOD

Christmas gives us a fresh, new understanding of what God is like. You see, this is the good news of Christmas: Jesus comes to show us what God is really like, and the picture he paints is the portrait of love.

Before Jesus came, people had only vague, shadowy, and often quite wrong ideas about God. God was sometimes depicted as harsh, hostile, vengeful, vindictive; but Jesus came to show us that God is love.

When I was about nine years old and living in Memphis, there was an older man in our neighborhood named Toby. He was an Italian farmer with long gray hair and a shaggy beard. He wore the clothes of a hard-working farmer—dirty overalls, dusty boots, a gray, sweat-stained hat—and his face looked like leather. He lived alone, the closest thing to a hermit I ever knew. He had very few social contacts, but he did buy his groceries at our little neighborhood store. My brother, Bob, who was eleven; my sister, Susie, who was three; and I, at age nine, were scared to death of Mr. Toby. It was said that Mr. Toby didn't like children. He didn't look like he would, and we weren't about to ask him. To us, he was scary, and we steered clear of him. As a matter of fact, every time Mr. Toby came around, the three of us (my brother, my sister, and I) would run and hide behind the hedge, and there, panic-stricken, we would wait in silence, shaking with fear, until Mr. Toby was out of sight again. We were so afraid of him that we actually had nightmares about him.

Then one day we saw Mr. Toby in a new light. We were playing in the yard when our pet cat was hit by a car. The cat came limping into the yard, dragging his back right leg. It was fractured. The three of us children were on our knees over the cat, crying and petting him. We were so upset that we didn't hear someone walk up.

Suddenly, our eyes fell on two dusty old boots. We looked up into the crusty face of Mr. Toby. Mr. Toby had a look of compassion in his eyes. He dropped to his knees and very tenderly gathered our injured cat into his arms and lovingly stroked him. Then, quick as a flash, he began barking out orders: "Susie, go get a towel. Bob, you get some tape. And Jim, you go to the store and bring me two Popsicle sticks."

When we returned with the supplies he had requested, Mr. Toby was holding the cat in his arms, rocking him like a baby and singing a soothing lullaby to him. A trace of tears had streamed down into his beard. He made a nice, neat splint for the cat's leg, then covered him with the towel and took him into our house and laid him in his cat bed. Then he went to the store and came back with three pieces of bubble gum. As he gave us the gum, he said, "I know about animals. Don't you kids worry now. Your cat's gonna be all right." With a smile and a wink, he turned and walked away.

And do you know what? We weren't ever afraid of Mr. Toby again. We didn't hide from him anymore. In fact, we became great friends. We had a whole new perception of him—a new picture, a new relationship, not one built on fear, but now one of love. That experience helped us children see him as he really was, and we loved him from that day on.

This may well be the best gift Christmas gives to us—a new picture of God, a new understanding of what God is really like, a new experience of God's compassion and tenderness, a new relationship with God built not on fear, but on love.

❧ ❧ ❧ ❧ ❧

SECOND, CHRISTMAS GIVES US
A NEW PARTNERSHIP WITH OTHERS

Christmas gives us not only a new way of seeing God but also a new way of looking at others—a new respect, a new regard for other people.

Christmas shows us that people are more important than things and that people are not pawns to be used, but persons to be loved, yes, children of God. Also, Christmas shows us that the best way to love God is to love God's children.

What better way to express this than with the powerful Christmas story entitled "The Fourth Wise Man." Remember the story? The fourth wise man was called Artaban. He, too, set out to follow the star, and he took with him three gifts—a sapphire, a ruby, and a pearl—all priceless gifts for the newborn king. He was riding hard to meet his three friends at the agreed-upon place. The time was short. The other three wise men would leave if he were late. Suddenly, Artaban saw a dim figure on the ground before him. It was a traveler stricken with fever. What should Artaban do? If he stayed to help, he would surely miss his friends, and they would go on without him. Artaban decided to stay and help the sick man. But now he was alone. He needed camels and bearers to help him cross the desert because he had missed his friends (the other three wise men) and their caravan. So he had to sell his sapphire to get them; and Artaban was sad because the King of kings would never receive the sapphire.

He journeyed on and in due time came to Bethlehem, but again he was too late. Joseph and Mary and the baby had gone to escape the devious plot of Herod to kill all the children. Artaban was in a house in Bethlehem where there was a little child. Soldiers came to the door. The weeping of the stricken mother could be heard across the darkness. Artaban stood in the doorway, tall and powerful. With the ruby in his hand he bribed the captain not to enter. The child was saved, the mother was overjoyed, but now the ruby was gone;

and Artaban was sad because the King of kings would never receive the ruby.

For years and years, Artaban wandered, looking in vain for the King. More than thirty years passed, and then Artaban came to Jerusalem. A crucifixion was to take place. When Artaban heard about this Jesus of Nazareth who was to be crucified, Artaban instinctively recognized that he was the one. Jesus was the King he had been searching for all those years. Artaban hurried toward Calvary. Maybe his pearl (the most precious in the world), his last gift, could buy the life of the King. But as he rushed toward Golgotha, Artaban came upon a young girl running away from a band of soldiers. "Please help me," she cried. "My father is in debt and they are taking me to sell as a slave to pay the debt. Please save me!" Artaban hesitated; then sadly he took out the pearl and gave it to the soldiers to buy the girl's freedom.

Now his last gift for the King was gone. Suddenly, there was an earthquake and Artaban was critically injured by some flying debris. He sank half-conscious and dying to the ground. Then like a whisper from very far away, there came a voice, "Verily I say to you, Artaban. Inasmuch as you have done it to one of the least of these my brethren, you have done it unto me." And Artaban smiled, even as he died, because he knew the King had indeed received all his gifts.

Christmas gives us a new picture of God, and Christmas gives us a new partnership with others, a partnership that reminds us that the best way to serve God is to love God's children.

❧ ❧ ❧ ❧ ❧

THIRD, CHRISTMAS GIVES US
A NEW PURPOSE FOR LIVING

This new purpose, a new sense of direction, a new meaning for our lives, is to share in the Christmas story, to daily celebrate God's love and pass it on to others, to dedicate everything we do to God.

Have you ever wondered why we put tinsel on our Christmas trees? It goes back to a beautiful legend, a story for children of all ages. According to the story, Joseph and Mary and their new baby, Jesus, were on their way to Egypt trying to escape from Herod's soldiers. Evening came and they were tired, so they sought refuge and warmth in a cave. It was very cold, so cold that the ground was white with frost.

A little friendly spider saw the Christ Child and somehow wished that he might do something to help him or to keep him warm in the cold night. He decided to do the only thing he could. He spun a web across the entrance to the cave, to make a kind of curtain there, in hopes that the web might keep some of the cold night air out of the cave. Later that night some of Herod's soldiers looking for children to kill to carry out Herod's order, came to that place. They were about to burst into the cave, but the captain noticed the spider's web, covered now with frost and stretching right across the entrance to the cave. "Look, men," he said. "Here's a spider's web. It is quite unbroken, so there cannot possibly be anyone in the cave. No use searching here." So, the soldiers passed on by and left the Holy Family in peace, because a little spider had spun his web of love across the entrance to the cave.

And that, so it is said, is why to this day, we put tinsel like this on our Christmas trees. The glittering tinsel streamers stand for the spider's web, white with frost, stretched across the entrance of the cave on the way to Egypt. The spider had spun his web many times before, but this time it was dedicated to God and as a result it meant life.

This is our purpose for living: to bring life rather than death, joy rather than sadness, love rather than hate. Christmas has for us three very special gifts that I hope we will claim today—a new picture of God, a new partnership with others, and a new purpose for living.

❧ ❧

CHAPTER 11

Come on Home to the "Easter Perspective"

Scripture: John 20:11-18

Let me begin this chapter with three short stories. See if you can find the common thread that links them together.

The first story is about a young boy who lost his contact lens while playing basketball in his driveway. So, immediately the game was stopped, and everyone started looking for the lost lens. But no luck. They couldn't find it. Just then the boy's mother drove up. "Mom," said the boy, "I lost my contact lens. We looked and looked but we can't find it anywhere." The mother got down on her hands and knees; she crawled around the driveway, and in less than a minute she said, "Here it is! I found it." The boys were amazed. "How did you do that?" they asked. "We looked, and we couldn't find it." "Simple," Mom said. "You all were looking for a small piece of plastic. I was looking for $150.00!"

The second story is about a bachelor college professor who met his male bachelor colleagues for coffee one morning. "I have some good news and some bad news," he said to them. "First, the good news: a recent student survey shows that college coeds today find middle-aged men extremely attractive. The bad news is: they think middle-age is twenty-five!"

The third story revolves around something that happened to our family recently. We went out to breakfast. However, when we arrived at the popular restaurant, the parking lot was jam-packed. I had to back out and go down the street to find a parking place. Actually, we were only about seventy-five yards from the restaurant; but since we didn't get into the parking lot, it seemed far away. I was moaning and groaning and apologizing that we would have to walk so far, when someone in the group said, "You know, if we went to a ball game at Cowboys Stadium and got to park this close, we would feel lucky!" Indeed so.

The common thread in these three stories is the matter of perspective, the manner in which we look at things. One person looks at a glass of water and sees it half empty. Another looks and sees it half full. It's a matter of perspective. One person looks at a cross and sees a symbol of darkness and death. Another person looks at a cross and sees a symbol of life and victory. It's a matter of perspective.

That's what Easter does for us: it gives us a new perspective, a new way of looking at things, a new view of life and death, and a new understanding of the cross. When Mary Magdalene saw her Lord nailed to the cross on Good Friday, it looked evil and horrible and devastating. It was the symbol of death. But on Easter morning, she got a new perspective. Christ had come off the cross and out of the tomb. Now, looking at the cross with Easter eyes, she saw it as the symbol of life and love and amazing grace. Let me show you what I mean.

One of the most popular stories that came out of the Second World War was about some marines who were shipwrecked in the South Pacific. After days of floating in a life raft, finally they see land. "Land ahoy!" someone shouts. They are overjoyed! Their fears begin to be dispelled and they make their way to the shore. They kiss the ground and say prayers of gratitude to God for saving them. But then very quickly, they see signs of life on that island and they realize that they are not alone there. The island is inhabited—but by whom?

Immediately, they begin to wonder, *Are we safe here? We are weak and hungry and we have no weapons of defense. Will the people of this island welcome us warmly? Or will they kill us on sight?* One of the young marines climbs up a tall palm tree to see if he can scope out the island and get some indication of what they might expect from the islanders. Are they saved? Or are they doomed?

Suddenly, from the top of the palm tree, the young marine calls down to the others: "It's OK, fellas! It's OK! We're saved! I see a steeple with a cross on it!"

It's all right. There is kindness here. There is understanding and grace and love here. We're saved! "I see a steeple with a cross on it." Isn't that a powerful and wonderful true story? The sign of the cross meant salvation to those marines. It meant life! That's what it means for us too. We must never lose sight of the cross!

In his book *Jesus Christ and His Cross*, F. W. Dillistone talks about the importance of the cross in the Christian faith. He points out that other religions have their symbols, such as the crescent, the sickle, the lotus flower, the wheel, the sun's disc, the living flame, and so on, but that Christianity revolves around the cross. He also points out that when Christianity drifts away from the cross, it weakens itself, and when it stays near the cross, it finds strength.

Do you know why? Because the cross is the message of God, the truth of God, the victory of God, the gospel of God, acted out in human history. This is what the apostle Paul is talking about in 1 Corinthians. The word of the cross is folly to those who are perishing, but to us who are being saved it is the power of God.

Some years ago, someone asked Pavlova, the great Russian dancer, what she meant by a certain dance. "What are you saying in that dance?" She replied, "If it could be said in words, there would be no need to dance it." Precisely! Certain truths are too big for words. They have to be dramatized. They have to be acted out. And that's why the cross and the Resurrection are so important to us. There on the old rugged cross of Good Friday, and there at the empty tomb of Easter morning, God dramatized the message, God acted it out for us. Now this symbol, the sign of the cross, serves as a constant and powerful reminder of God's truth for us, God's will for us, and God's love for us. Let me put it in a simple outline that we can all easily remember. The cross is the symbol of faith, hope, and love. That's the way the apostle Paul sums it up, isn't it? Faith, hope, and love! I don't know how to improve on that, so let's take a look at these one at a time.

✤ ✤ ✤ ✤ ✤

FIRST, THE CROSS IS THE SYMBOL OF FAITH

What in the world does that mean? Basically, *faith* means that we can trust God. In the end, in God's own good time, God will win. And if we want to come out winners, we had best get on God's team. God is still God and God is still in charge of this world and the final victory will be God's. The cross reminds us of that. Now, let's be honest. Sometimes it does seem that sin and evil are on top. Sometimes it seems that they are overwhelming us. Sometimes it seems that they have all the steam and all the loudest arguments. But listen! God will win, and we can count on that. And God wants to share the victory with you and me.

The cross reminds us of that. It is a constant reminder of God's victory over sin and evil and wickedness. In Gounod's opera *Faust*, there is a dramatic scene where the Satan character gets into a sword fight with the young man, Valentine. In the course of the fight, Satan breaks the sword of Valentine and is about to run him through. But at the last second, young Valentine turns his broken sword upside down in the likeness of a cross, and the Satan character stands there paralyzed. Against the sign of the cross, the evil one is powerless. The cross is the symbol of faith because it reminds us of God's incredible victory over sin and evil and that victory is precisely what gives us the poise, the serenity, the confidence, and the blessed assurance we love to sing about.

One of the most moving scenes in all English literature comes at the close of Charles Dickens's *Tale of Two Cities*. The carts were rumbling through the crowded streets of Paris, heading toward the guillotine, where in the most ruthless, cruel way, people's heads would be chopped off in full view of the curious public. In one cart, riding to be executed, were two prisoners, a brave man who had lost his life but had found it again and was now laying it down for a friend, and beside him a young girl. They are riding toward their death, holding hands.

Earlier, in the prison, she had noticed the strength and calmness of his face and she had said to him, "If I may ride with you, will you let me hold your hand? I am so very small and it will give me courage." So, on this day as they ride together toward their place of execution, there is no fear in her eyes as she holds tightly to his hand. As they reach the guillotine, calmly she looks up into the strong face of the man beside her and says, "I think you were sent to me by heaven."

That is the good news of our faith. That is the message of the cross, the promise of Easter. One has been sent to us by heaven, and come what may he will give us strength and he will see us through. We can count on that. First of all, the cross is the sign of faith, the reminder that no matter what happens to us in this life, we can trust God.

🌿 🌿 🌿 🌿 🌿

SECOND, THE CROSS IS THE SYMBOL OF HOPE

If you have a pain today so great that you feel as though it will never go away, if you have a depression that you feel is so heavy that it can never be lifted, if there is a situation in your life right now in which you see no possible solution, then now is the time for you to especially remember the cross and to remember what Easter teaches us—that all trouble is temporary.

Painful Good Fridays do come for all of us, but in time they give way to the new life of Easter morning. Sometimes in this world we get knocked down, but the cross reminds us that we can rise again; we can have a new beginning, a new start, a new life.

Some months ago, I went to a home where a great tragedy had struck. This family had endured a lot of suffering over the years, and once again calamity had struck them. The father of that family hugged me and cried like a baby. Then he grew silent. Finally, he said, "Jim, I just don't know if I can stand this. I made it through the other things, but I don't see how I can make it through this one."

I was so glad that I could tell him that the Christian faith says: Oh, yes, you will! Yes, you will! God will bring you through this valley to the mountaintop on the other side. God has done it before, and God will do it again. Because nothing can separate us from God and God's love. And the cross reminds us that nothing, not even death, can defeat God. That is our faith, and that is our hope. The cross reminds us of that.

☙ ☙ ☙ ☙ ☙

THIRD, AND FINALLY, THE CROSS IS THE SYMBOL OF LOVE

Some years ago, a ten-year-old boy named Johnny was sitting alone on a park bench one afternoon. It was a beautiful spring day, and Johnny was watching some other children play baseball. An older man happened by. He saw Johnny sitting there, and he sat down beside him on the park bench. They started talking. They talked about the gorgeous weather, about sports, about their families. Finally, the older man said, "Johnny, I want to ask you a question. If you had three wishes, what would you wish for?" Johnny thought for a moment, and then he said, "First, I would wish for peace and happiness in the world. Second, I would wish everybody would join the church. And third, I would wish that my best friend Billy, who is blind, would be able to see. That's what I would wish for."

The older man seemed amazed by Johnny's answer, and, with a look of perplexity, the older man said good-bye and walked away. Johnny didn't understand why the man was confused and taken aback by his answer. He sat there for a moment, and then Johnny picked up his crutches and hobbled home.

You know where Johnny got that gracious, loving spirit, don't you? He got it from Jesus. He got it from the one who went to the cross for you and me. He got it from the one who came out of the tomb showing us that love is the most powerful thing in the world. On the cross, God shows us how much God loves us and how much God wants us to love one another.

Faith, hope, love—that's what the cross is about; and may Jesus keep us near the cross.

❧ ❧

Chapter 12

Come on Home to Christ's Understanding of Success

Scripture: Luke 19:28-40

Jesus came riding triumphantly into Jerusalem, the picture of success. Then, just a few days later, he was nailed to a cross like a common criminal. What happened? What do we make of this? Was Jesus a success? What do you think?

For many years now, we in America have been highly "success conscious," "success oriented." And most of us have agreed with *Webster's* definition: "the attainment of wealth, favor, or eminence." Think about it. Isn't it true that when we think of success we immediately pull out names like Rockefeller, Kennedy, Ford, DuPont, or Trump? They symbolize the "sweet smell of success." But, Webster was wrong. Money and fame are not enough. In fact, some who look highly successful are actually quite miserable.

Some years ago, a well-dressed young man came to a priest in Paris for counseling. He complained of being blue, unfulfilled, and depressed. The old priest said to the young man, "Go to Grimaldi; he is the handsome, young, happy-go-lucky leader of the continental jet set. He is the life of every party. His frivolous good times are legendary all over Europe. He is known far and wide for his joyous exploits. The whole world envies Grimaldi. Yes," said the priest, "go to Grimaldi. He will show you how to be happy." "But sir," said the young man, "I AM Grimaldi."

You see, there is more to successful living than partying, eating well, and counting wealth. Our customary standards of measuring success are shoddy and shallow. How much money do you make? How many cars do you have? When was the last time you had breakfast in Paris, my dear? The very questions reflect a poverty of soul and a gross misunderstanding of what genuine success is really all about.

To get into this a little deeper, let's telescope in on that dramatic scene in the Gospels where Jesus stands before Pontius Pilate (see John 18:28–19:16). What a contrast. How different these two men are!

Notice something here. If you asked some folk today who knew nothing of the story to point out the successful one in this scene—

using our present-day standards for measuring success—they would point quickly to Pontius Pilate. And they would document their choice by underscoring Pilate's wealth, his position, his power, his authority, his political clout, his fame—and yet they would be wrong. So very wrong.

In Jesus, we see a whole new, different understanding of what success is. His approach is so different that it startles us. In effect, he says, "If you want to be great or successful, then be a servant." "Be a servant?" What on earth can Jesus mean by that? Successful people aren't servants. "Successful people have servants," we cry out. What is he trying to do, upset our whole scale of values? Well, yes, that is precisely what he is trying to do, to give us a whole new scale of values, a new measuring stick, a new standard for measuring success.

Now, with that as a backdrop, let's look together at some of the qualities of life that seemed of great importance to Jesus, the qualities that make for real success.

❧ ❧ ❧ ❧ ❧

SUCCESS IS NOT SO MUCH IN OUTER CIRCUMSTANCES AS IT IS IN INNER STABILITY, INNER PEACE, AND STRENGTH

Look at the scene with Pilate again in light of that. Who has the inner peace and strength here? Pilate has the outer circumstances but not the inner stability. Jesus is the strong one here. In fact, his inner strength baffles Pilate.

Look at Pilate here. He is confused, upset, weak. He can't make up his mind. In a dither, he runs from one group to the other, asking questions here and there. He tries to pass the buck to Herod. He knows that Jesus is innocent, but Pilate does not have the strength of character to stand firm for what is right. This is the picture of a man who is running scared.

Outwardly Pilate has it all—power, wealth, position, and fame—but inwardly, where it really counts, he is scared to death. Finally, he washes his hands (Matthew 27:24), and tries to straddle the fence. Nervously, he gives the people what they want, he turns Jesus over to them for execution, but then just in case someone else may see it differently, he tries to act as if he is not really involved. Is that success? Is being scared, confused, and weak "success"? Surely not.

On the other side of the coin, look at Jesus. He stands there poised, confident, and unafraid. He is facing death, but his strength never wavers. Just think of it, an unfair trial for an innocent man, lies, plotting, conniving, bribed witnesses, political intrigue, jealousy, hostility, hatred, a mob scene—and in the face of it all, Jesus exhibits an amazing quality of inner peace and strength and calm.

They betray him, deny him, taunt him, beat him, curse him, spit upon him, and nail him to a cross. And he says: "Father, forgive them; for they do not know what they are doing" (Luke 23:34). Now, that is strength of character, isn't it? That is inner peace. That is real success. Real success is not so much in outer circumstances as it is in inner stability. In that regard Jesus was the most successful man who ever lived.

How lacking are these qualities of peace and inner strength in our world today. People chain-smoke, knowing the consequences, because they are nervous within. People become habitual drinkers, knowing the consequences, because they are restless within. People drug themselves, tranquilize themselves, because the mounting pressures of life have torn their inner world to shreds. Some people would give anything for a good night's rest, for a sense of peace within. Jesus offers it to us: "Peace I leave with you; my peace I give to you" (John 14:27).

This, for the Christian, is the source of calm and inner strength. It was the contagion of this confidence that enabled those early Christians to stand unflinchingly against horrible persecution, to sing hymns of praise in prison cells, and to face death with courage and poise. Their inner lives were strong, secure, peaceful. Their inner lives were successful; that is the only success that really matters. Real success is not out there. It's in here, in the heart.

✣ ✣ ✣ ✣ ✣

SUCCESS IS NOT SO MUCH IN HAVING MANY POSSESSIONS AS IT IS IN PURSUING A DREAM

Real success lies in giving your life to and for something bigger than you are. A dream, a cause, a purpose, a ministry—that's more important than all the money and all the material possessions in the world.

Once I visited a successful businessman in his luxurious office suite. It was magnificent, elegant, perfectly and expensively furnished. He showed me into his private office, closed the door, and said, "Jim, I have everything I have ever dreamed of having and more. I have wealth, power, authority. I have a fine home, three luxury cars, money to do anything I want to do. I have a lovely wife, wonderful children, a respected profession, I'm in good health. Despite all that I am miserable. I feel empty inside, unfulfilled; I am bored to tears. People call me a success, but I feel like a failure." What that man was saying was that he has everything but a cause, everything but a dream—and without that his life is an empty shell.

When *Man of La Mancha* came to Broadway in March of 1968, there was not much excitement. Nobody expected much. It was only another staging of the old Don Quixote story. The opening night audience came—not expecting much, not overly excited. But, you know what happened? When the final curtain came down, the audience as one came up to a resounding, roof-raising, standing ovation! The people cheered, shouted, applauded; some were moved to tears. The critics raved, calling it a musical that would last for generations. Why? Because the words and music tugged at something buried deep down in the human heart, something that most people thought dead and gone forever. It was the appeal of a great dream, the challenge of striving after some tremendous ideal.

Jesus knew about that important longing deep within us, and in the Sermon on the Mount he underscored it by saying, "Seek first [God's] kingdom and his righteousness, and all these things will be given to you as well" (Matthew 6:33 NIV). "Blessed are those who [keep on hungering and thirsting after righteousness], for they will be filled" (5:6 NIV).

Patrick Henry knew the importance of pursuing a great dream, and he closed his will with these words: "I have now disposed of all my property to my family. There is one thing more that I wish I could give them and that is the Christian faith. If they had this and I had not given them one shilling, they would be rich; and if they had not that and I had given them all the world, they would be poor." Success comes not from material possessions. Success comes from giving your life to a great dream.

❧ ❧ ❧ ❧ ❧

SUCCESS IS NOT LIVING FOR SELF; IT IS LIVING FOR OTHERS

The little boy came home from Sunday school. He had studied the parable of the good Samaritan. When someone asked, "What did you learn?" he replied, "I learned that when I'm in trouble, somebody ought to help me." He missed the whole point; and so often, so do we.

By present-day standards of success, Jesus wouldn't measure up so well. He was born in a stable. His mother was a peasant girl; his father a carpenter. Jesus had little formal schooling, wrote no books, held no offices, claimed no political fame. He travelled very little. He taught, but many scoffed at his teaching. His closest friends betrayed him. And then almost before the story got started, he was nailed to a cross like a common criminal and put to death.

That doesn't sound like a success story, does it? Yet two thousand years later, people bow at his name and look in amazement at his perceptive teaching. People's lives are changed because of him. Why? Because he showed us what God is like and what God wants us to become, and the word is *LOVE*. He who is greatest and most successful among you must be a servant, a servant of God, of people, of love.

Some years ago, we had the privilege of worshiping in a Christian church in Guilin, China. It was packed with worshipers. We came to church unannounced, and the people accepted us warmly in the Spirit of Christ. The minister preached a three-point sermon in Chinese, and, though we couldn't understand all of what he was saying, we got the drift of it. He was lifting up Jesus Christ as the Lord of life and the Savior of the world. After the sermon, we stood and sang the closing hymn, "More Love to Thee, O Christ, More Love to Thee." They sang in Chinese and we sang in English. Think of it. There we were, twelve thousand miles from home, singing that familiar hymn with that Chinese congregation. Some of us were holding our hymnals upside down, but we were singing the hymn together powerfully. And it dawned on me in a fresh, new way—the incredible impact of Jesus Christ on this world.

So, if you want to be a success, accept Christ into your heart as your personal Savior and know the inner strength that comes from that. If you want to be a success, catch hold of his dream and commit your life to that dream. If you want to be a success, live every day, every moment as a servant of Christ's love. That's what it's all about: being at home with God and being at home with others.

✤ ✤ ✤ ✤ ✤ ✤ ✤ ✤ ✤ ✤ ✤ ✤ ✤ ✤ ✤ ✤ ✤ ✤ ✤ ✤

Discussion Guide

for James W. Moore's
Come on Home: Healing the Homesickness of the Soul

John D. Schroeder

CHAPTER 1

Come on Home to Faith

SNAPSHOT SUMMARY

This chapter presents three true stories that show the meaning of a living faith through church, grace, and love.

REFLECTION/DISCUSSION QUESTIONS

1. Share a time when you realized the power of communication.
2. What impresses you about Helen Keller? What can we learn from her life story?
3. Why is it important to know words and names of faith?

4. How did you feel after reading the first story? What did it tell you about church?

5. Discuss how the names of church and faith are connected.

6. In your own words, explain the meaning of grace.

7. What do we learn about grace from the second story?

8. Share a time when you experienced the power of love.

9. Discuss how Romans 12 ties together church, grace, and love.

10. What additional thoughts or questions from this chapter would you like to explore?

ACTIVITIES

As a group: Ask each person to use his or her Bible to locate a favorite verse about faith and to share why it is meaningful.

OR

Ask each member to draw a picture of his or her home and to fill it with words of faith.

At home: Reflect upon your faith journey. How did it begin? When was your faith the strongest and the weakest? What helped you grow your faith? Where do you want to be a year from now?

Prayer: *Dear God, thank you for a living faith, fueled by grace, love, and the church. Help us grow in faith. Show us how to focus on loving and serving you by loving and serving others. Amen.*

CHAPTER 2

Come on Home to God's Greatest Promise

SNAPSHOT SUMMARY

This chapter reminds us that God meets us at every corner with loving-kindness. God meets us in times of rejection and trouble, and is there with us in death.

REFLECTION/DISCUSSION QUESTIONS

1. Share how you learned about God when you were a child.
2. Discuss Psalm 59:10 and how it ministers to us.
3. How are Psalm 59:10 and Psalm 139 connected?
4. Discuss how Psalm 139 encourages you. After reading it, how does it make you feel?
5. Name some times and places of rejection in life.
6. When facing rejection, how should you respond?
7. Share a time when you found yourself in a place of trouble and how God was there for you.
8. Discuss "Footprints" and what we can learn from it.
9. God is with us in death. How do we know it? Share your thoughts and experiences.
10. What additional thoughts and questions from this chapter would you like to explore?

ACTIVITIES

As a group: Give each member a pencil and paper. Ask them to draw a corner with God on one side and a list of troubles on the other side. Share your drawings.

OR

Give each member the materials to create a bookmark containing words or messages from this lesson.

At home: This week, take time to remember the promises of God and how God has been there for you at every corner. Look for God in action in your life this week.

Prayer: *Dear God, thank you for the promises you have made to us. You are always with us in times of rejection and trouble, and even in death. Nothing can separate us from your love. Help us remember your constant love and presence. Amen.*

CHAPTER 3

Come on Home to Commitment

SNAPSHOT SUMMARY

This chapter explores the topic of commitment by examining the danger of the Teflon mind, the power of commitment, and the best tribute we can pay Jesus Christ.

REFLECTION/DISCUSSION QUESTIONS

1. Share a time when you struggled with the issue of commitment.
2. Discuss and describe "Teflon minds" and their dangers.
3. Why do some lessons, principles, and great truths stick with us but others don't?
4. Discuss Romans 12:1-2. Why is it powerful?
5. In your own words, what does making a commitment mean to you?
6. How do you commit your life to God and God's truth? Name some words and deeds that demonstrate commitment.
7. Discuss what it means to live sacrificially for God.
8. Brainstorm ways to pay tribute to Jesus.

9. If you want to "catch the pass," what do you need to do?

10. What additional thoughts or questions from this chapter would you like to explore?

ACTIVITIES

As a group: Ask each member to create his or her own personal commitment card, stating his or her commitments, promises, and loyalty.

OR

As a group, search the Bible for verses and examples of commitment.

At home: Evaluate your commitments this week to God and others. Examine what is important and what is not. Do you need to renew commitments or make any new ones?

Prayer: *Dear God, thank you for your commitment to us, from our birth and through eternity. Help us avoid the dangers of the Teflon mind, stand by our commitments to you and others, and daily pay tribute to Jesus as best we can. Amen.*

CHAPTER 4

Come on Home to the Christian Lifestyle

SNAPSHOT SUMMARY

This chapter looks at saints and saintly qualities and encourages us to live a Christian lifestyle. It reminds us that real saints have a sense of direction, a sense of love, and a sense of commitment.

REFLECTION/DISCUSSION QUESTIONS

1. In your own words, what does it mean to have a Christian lifestyle?

2. Discuss why Christianity is more than believing.

3. Name some reasons people fail to practice what they preach.

4. Discuss what "Christians are called to be stepping-stones" means.

5. Define what it means to be a saint.

6. Why is it important to have a sense of direction? Give an example.

7. Share a time when you experienced a sense of love.

8. How do you become a saint?

9. Discuss how commitment begins or is obtained.

10. What additional thoughts or questions from this chapter would you like to explore?

ACTIVITIES

As a group: Create a group list of some saintly things to do for others.

OR

Ask the group members to write down two ideas from this lesson that made an impact on them. Have them explain why these ideas are important.

At home: Look at and evaluate your own lifestyle. Consider strengths and weaknesses of how you live as a Christian. Is your faith reflected in how you live and act? Where is there room for improvement?

Prayer: *Dear God, thank you for saints and our ability to live saintly lives. Grant us the sense of direction, love, and commitment we need to minister in your name. Show us how to live and how to dedicate our lives to you and others. Amen.*

CHAPTER 5

Come on Home to the Atmosphere of Christ

SNAPSHOT SUMMARY

This chapter explores the words of Paul about living your life totally for God, in your own atmosphere. It shows us why it is important to take commitment, trust in God, and love for God on our journey through life.

REFLECTION/DISCUSSION QUESTIONS

1. What is meant by taking your own atmosphere with you?
2. Discuss how you can be transformed by the renewal of your mind.
3. List some of the ways that the world squeezes you into its mold.
4. Share a time when you faced an ethical decision. How do you make tough decisions?
5. Discuss the origins of making a commitment to God. How do they begin?
6. What qualities are needed in order to maintain a commitment?
7. Share a time when you trusted in God.
8. In your own words, what does it mean to trust God?
9. How do we demonstrate love for God? List some ways or ideas.
10. What additional thoughts or questions from this chapter would you like to explore?

ACTIVITIES

As a group: Give each member the resources to draw a picture of the atmosphere of Christ. Share and explain your creations.

OR

Ask each group member to create his or her own list of foods for the soul. Name some cans of soul food each person should take along for nourishment on life's journey.

At home: Reflect upon the three topics of commitment, trust, and love. Are you living in the atmosphere of Christ? Are you getting enough nourishment?

Prayer: *Dear God, thank you for Paul's message to us on how to live our lives for you. Help us avoid the dangers of this world and show us how to live lives of commitment, trust, and love. Amen.*

CHAPTER 6

Come on Home to Christ's Healing

SNAPSHOT SUMMARY

This chapter reminds us how we can become bent out of shape as nations, as families, and as persons. It shows us the constant need for Christ's healing in our lives.

REFLECTION/DISCUSSION QUESTIONS

1. Share a time when you got bent out of shape and needed healing.
2. What lessons can we learn from the Luke 13 story of Jesus and the woman with a back problem?
3. List some of the qualities that Jesus displayed in his ministry to this woman.
4. Name a time when our nation was bent out of shape.
5. How does our nation's drug problem affect us all?
6. List some of the problems we struggle with as a nation. What are the top two?
7. Discuss the ways that families become bent out of shape.

8. What often causes you to get bent out of shape?

9. List some cures or remedies to help people who are bent out of shape.

10. What additional thoughts or questions from this chapter would you like to explore?

ACTIVITIES

As a group: Ask each member to list the ingredients of a "Shape-up Kit" for individuals. What is in it? Share your lists.

OR

Locate Bible verses that promote healing. Create a group list. Have members copy them down for future reference.

At home: This week, consider what kind of shape you are in spiritually. Think about what causes you to get bent out of shape and ways to come home to Christ's healing.

Prayer: *Dear God, thank you for your healing touch. Please continue to bless us and touch our nation, our families, and ourselves with your presence and healing. Help us remember the needs of others and show our love to them. Amen.*

Chapter 7

Come on Home to Servanthood

SNAPSHOT SUMMARY

This chapter shows us the true meaning of being a servant. It warns us against having a spirit of arrogance, hostility, and resentment.

REFLECTION/DISCUSSION QUESTIONS

1. In your own words, explain what it means to be a servant.

2. What qualities does a good servant possess?

3. Why is *chosen* a good word gone bad?

4. Discuss the statement "Service is the key to happiness because it is the call of God."

5. Why do we, like the disciples, often have trouble grasping the servant concept?

6. How does arrogance begin? Name some strategies to make it end.

7. Discuss how hostility taints the soul.

8. Share a time you experienced resentment—given or received.

9. Brainstorm ways to remind yourself daily that you are a servant.

10. What additional thoughts or ideas from this chapter would you like to explore?

ACTIVITIES

As a group: Give each group member the resources to create his or her own personalized certificate of servanthood with his or her name on it. Show your certificates to one another.

OR

Serve a meal at a homeless shelter or perform as a group some act of service.

At home: Take a look at your track record of service to others. Look for room for improvement. How can you become a more effective servant?

Prayer: *Dear God, thank you for giving us the opportunity to serve you and others. Help us grasp the concept of what it means to be a servant. Lead us to needs and to ways we can help others. Amen.*

CHAPTER 8

Come on Home to the Spirit of Gratitude

SNAPSHOT SUMMARY

This chapter uses the story of Jesus and Zacchaeus to help us learn more about the true spirit of gratitude. It shows us how Christ gave Zacchaeus—and gives us—new priorities, a new appreciation, and a new motivation.

REFLECTION/DISCUSSION QUESTIONS

1. Share a time when you experienced the real spirit of thanksgiving.

2. Name some reasons we fail to see all of our blessings.

3. What lessons can be learned from the story of Jesus and Zacchaeus?

4. Explain why real thanksgiving changes our lives.

5. Discuss how we can receive the new appreciation that Jesus gave to Zacchaeus.

6. Christianity is by definition thanksgiving. Discuss this truth and explain it.

7. When are you the most appreciative? When are you the least appreciative?

8. Discuss some signs that you need new or better priorities.

9. What motivates most people? As Christians, what should motivate us?

10. What additional thoughts or questions from this chapter would you like to explore?

ACTIVITIES

As a group: Create a group list of some easy ways to develop a better spirit of gratitude.

OR

Ask each member to write down a list of what he or she is most thankful for. Share and compare lists. Any similarities?

At home: Show your grateful side this week. Look for opportunities to show to family and friends that you know how blessed you really are. Practice being thankful.

Prayer: *Dear God, thank you for giving us the story of Zacchaeus to show what it means to live in a spirit of gratitude. Grant us what you gave Zacchaeus: a new acceptance, a new evaluation, and a new motivation. Amen.*

CHAPTER 9

Come on Home to Generosity

SNAPSHOT SUMMARY

This chapter shows us the three types of Christian givers and encourages us to be generous to others. It is our turn and our opportunity to give of ourselves.

REFLECTION/DISCUSSION QUESTIONS

1. Share a time when you were the recipient of someone's generosity.
2. Name some reasons we fail to give or be generous.
3. Discuss why out of the thirty major parables, twenty of them relate to our possessions and our giving.
4. God loves a cheerful giver. List more words that should reflect our attitude toward giving.
5. Explain griot giving and give an example of it.
6. Discuss how grateful givers are different from griot givers. Do they have any similarities?

7. Why should the church be at the top of our list in our giving?

8. How do generous givers view money, and why are they so generous?

9. List some steps to take to become more generous. How do you begin?

10. What additional thoughts or questions from this chapter would you like to explore?

ACTIVITIES

As a group: Give the group members empty, clean aluminum cans and the resources to create their own "giving banks." They will use them to collect spare change to give away. Ask them to decorate their banks with words from this lesson.

OR

Ask each member to take a dollar bill from his or her wallet or purse and write a brief sentence on it about giving. The bill can be kept as a reminder or spent. A plain piece of paper can also be used for this activity.

At home: Show your generous side this week. Look for opportunities to give of your time, talents, and money. Strive to be a better giver!

Prayer: *Dear God, thank you for being so generous with us. We are truly blessed. Help us to be generous to others. Show us opportunities to give of ourselves. Amen.*

CHAPTER 10

Come on Home to the Good News of Christmas

SNAPSHOT SUMMARY

This chapter reminds us of the real meaning of Christmas. It shows us the three special gifts we can claim today: a new picture of God, a new partnership with others, and a new purpose for living.

REFLECTION/DISCUSSION QUESTIONS

1. Share a Christmas memory and explain why it is so special to you.
2. List some of the gifts that Christmas gives us.
3. Why do we often miss the gifts of Christmas?
4. Discuss how Christmas gives us a new picture of God.
5. What does it mean to have a new partnership with others? Why are new partnerships important?
6. How can each day be Christmas? Brainstorm some ideas.
7. Name some of the ways Christmas gives us a new purpose for living.
8. List some ways we can appreciate others more and treat them as gifts.
9. What do we need to do in order to claim the special gifts of Christmas?
10. What additional thoughts or questions from this chapter would you like to explore?

ACTIVITIES

As a group: Have your own Christmas celebration, complete with food, presents, hymns, and handmade decorations.

OR

Create a "top ten" list of why people are more important than things.

At home: Get in the Christmas spirit. Place a Christmas decoration in the living room. Give gifts of your time and talents. Listen to a hymn. Reflect on the true meaning and gifts of Christmas.

Prayer: *Dear God, thank you for the good news and blessings of Christmas. Help us celebrate Christmas in our hearts each day of the year. Open our eyes and ears to how you want us to bring the joys of Christmas to others. Amen.*

CHAPTER 11

Come on Home to the "Easter Perspective"

SNAPSHOT SUMMARY

This chapter shows how important perspective is when we look at Easter and all aspects of our lives. It reminds us that the cross is a symbol of faith, hope, and love.

REFLECTION/DISCUSSION QUESTIONS

1. Share a time when you found something was a matter of perspective.
2. Discuss how and why Easter gives us a new perspective.
3. People see different things when looking at a cross. Name some things they see. What do you see and feel?
4. Discuss why the cross is a symbol of faith for us.
5. What does the cross remind us of and why is it so powerful?
6. Share a time when you got "knocked down." How did the cross remind you to rise again?
7. Discuss the times in life when the cross serves as a symbol of hope for us.
8. How has your perspective of the cross changed as you have grown older?
9. Discuss the cross as a powerful symbol of love.
10. What additional thoughts or questions from this chapter would you like to explore?

ACTIVITIES

As a group: Ask each member to draw an Easter basket and fill it with words and symbols of Easter.

OR

Go on an Easter word hunt in the Bible. Search for the words *faith, hope,* and *love.* Each member should find five verses to share.

At home: Observe Easter in spirit this week and reflect on its meaning to you. Look for symbols of Easter during your week.

Prayer: *Dear God, thank you for the gift of Easter and hope, faith, and love, which draws us closer to you and others. Help us cherish the meaning of Easter and observe it in spirit all year long. Amen.*

CHAPTER 12

Come on Home to Christ's Understanding of Success

SNAPSHOT SUMMARY

This chapter examines success as Christ views it. The qualities that make for real success are inner stability, inner peace, and inner strength. Second, success is not having possessions but pursuing dreams. And success is not living for self. It is living for others.

REFLECTION/DISCUSSION QUESTIONS

1. Share a time when you enjoyed well-deserved success.
2. Discuss how the appearance of success can be misleading.
3. How would Jesus define success?
4. Discuss how the world measures success. How does it miss the mark?
5. How do you obtain inner stability, inner peace, and inner strength? Why do many people lack these qualities?

6. Discuss and contrast Pilate and Jesus. Why was Jesus stronger than Pilate?

7. Share your insights on the value of pursuing a dream.

8. Discuss the importance of living for others.

9. How would you define genuine success?

10. What additional thoughts or questions from this chapter would you like to explore?

ACTIVITIES

As a group: Celebrate the conclusion of this small group experience with a graduation party.

OR

Ask each member to create a bumper sticker on the topic of success.

At home: Reflect upon this small group experience. What have you learned and gained? Where do you go from here?

Prayer: *Dear God, thank you for giving us a clearer understanding of real success. Thank you for this group experience. Bless each member and be with us always. Amen.*